D0757350

Change Your Mind
—and Keep the Change

Advanced NLP Submodalities Inverventions

by
Connirae Andreas
and
Steve Andreas

with the editorial assistance of
Michael Eric Bennett *and* Donna Wilson

REAL PEOPLE PRESS / MOAB, UTAH 84532

Copyright © 1987
Real People Press
Box F
Moab, UT 84532

ISBN: 0-911226-28-1 clothbound $12.00
ISBN: 0-911226-29-X paperbound $ 8.50

Cover by Rene Eisenbart

Library of Congress Cataloging in Publication Data

Andreas, Connirae
    Change your mind—and keep the change.

    Bibliography: p.
    Includes index.
    1. Neurolinguistic programming. I. Andreas,
Steve. II. Title.
BF637.N46A53 1987   158'.1   87-24327
ISBN 0-911226-28-1
ISBN 0-911226-29-X (pbk.)

Other books about Neuro-Linguistic Programming from **Real People Press:**

FROGS INTO PRINCES, by *Richard Bandler and John Grinder*. 197 pp. 1979. Cloth $11.00, Paper $7.50.

USING YOUR BRAIN—FOR A CHANGE, by *Richard Bandler*. 159 pp. 1985. Cloth $11.00, Paper $7.50.

REFRAMING: Neuro-Linguistic Programming and the Transformation of Meaning, by *Richard Bandler and John Grinder*. 220 pp. 1981. Cloth $12.00, Paper $8.50.

TRANCE-FORMATIONS: Neuro-Linguistic Programming and the Structure of Hypnosis, by *John Grinder and Richard Bandler*. 250 pp. 1981. Cloth $12.00, Paper $8.50.

The name *Real People Press* indicates our purpose; to publish information and methods that a person can use independently or with others to become more *real*—to further your own growth as a human being and to develop your relationships and communication with others.

1 2 3 4 5 6 7 8 9 10 Printing 92 91 90 89 88 87

Contents

health" "responding to others' needs" are not important enough. Submodalities can be used to rapidly change how important something is to you.

V. *Eliminating Compulsions*   89-114
Strong responses such as eating compulsions, anger, addictions, etc. that don't respond to other methods often can be changed quickly with the compulsion blowout, followed by a swish.

VI. *"The Last Straw" Threshold Pattern*   115-132
How to get someone out of a destructive behavior or relationship.

VII. *Internal/External Reference*   133-146
Some people "naturally" decide for themselves, while others are easily impressed and swayed by the opinions of others. Use this information to help people make their own decisions.

VIII. *A Strategy for Responding to Criticism*   147-162
A step-by-step procedure used by those who naturally respond well to criticism. Learn to stay in a resourceful state while you evaluate criticism and decide how you can use the "feedback" to improve your behavior in the future.

IX. *Accessing Kinesthetic States*   163-178
Bringing back drug states can be more than just entertainment. This method has been utilized by people needing anesthetic or pain-killers, but not wanting the negative side-effects of actually taking the drugs. The method can be used for any state with a strong kinesthetic component.

X. *Other Submodality Interventions*   179-188
Specific "Briefest Therapy" interventions to change your mind. Modelling excellence.

Foreword

Steve and Connirae Andreas came to their first NLP Seminar with me in fall of 1977, nearly 10 years ago. Since then they have consistently demonstrated their tenacity in taking the patterns I teach and using them repeatedly until they understand them thoroughly. Chapter 3 on The Swish Pattern demonstrates how they can take a specific pattern and then explore it thoroughly to determine the essential pieces that make it work, as well as how to adapt the pattern to unusual or difficult cases.

Most of my students tell me about their successes with the patterns I teach. In contrast, Connirae and Steve tell me about their failures, because those are much more interesting to them. Successes are boring, because they only confirm what you already know. Failures are much more interesting, because they indicate where you can learn something new. Their fascination with the variety of subjective experience, and the regularities that underlie that variety, shows in the quality of the NLP trainings they have been offering over the last eight years. Their teaching is widely known for its integrity, ecology, and attention to detail, and this is also clearly reflected in this book.

Most NLP students are content if they master the patterns that have already been developed. One of my greatest pleasures is having someone learn not only the specific patterns that I teach, but the perceptions, attitudes, and thinking processes that create those patterns. Steve and Connirae are among the few who have gone on to use NLP modeling techniques to develop useful new patterns, and this, too, is evident in this book. Chapter 8, "A Strategy for Responding to Criticism," demonstrates their ability to model an essential skill—openness to feedback—and distill it into a clean and elegant syntax.

This book is an excellent sequel to my book *Using Your Brain—for a CHANGE*, which the Andreas created from audiotapes of my seminars, and it is my pleasure to recommend this book to anyone who wants to further explore how to change your mind.

—Richard Bandler

Acknowledgements

This book, and much of our recent work, would not exist without the creative genius of Richard Bandler. We are grateful to him for repeatedly providing us with new methods that can be used to make people's lives better, and tantalizing us with demonstrations, hints, and cryptic descriptions. Many of the patterns presented here were developed by Richard: The Compulsion Blowout, "The Last Straw" Threshold Pattern, The Swish Pattern, The Godiva Chocolate Pattern, and the utilization of verb tense shifts.

We have developed the other submodality patterns presented here by utilizing submodality principles we learned from Richard. We were so excited by the power of what he taught us that we began to ask ourselves, "What else can we apply this to?" We began to explore how people organize and represent events in relation to Timelines, Changing Criteria, Internal/External Reference, and developed the Strategy for Responding to Criticism.

Although we learned the Kinesthetic State Access pattern from Richard Bandler, Ed Reese first developed it. We have added the redesign steps to this pattern.

We would also like to acknowledge the many workshop participants and clients who have helped us over the last three years of exploring these patterns. They have made interesting observations, posed tough questions, found unique ways to carry out our instructions, and provided us with fascinating examples of the incredible variety of ways to organize subjective experience.

Finally we are glad to acknowledge the considerable editorial help of

Michael Eric Bennett and Donna Wilson, who prepared early versions of most of the chapters from transcripts of our seminars, and who carefully reviewed the final manuscript. Their work enabled us to make this material available in book form much more rapidly than we could have working alone.

Introduction

Our favorite story about the appropriate usefulness of words comes from an experience we had in California at a party in the mid-70's. We went with a friend of ours named Mike, who arrived at the party quite hungry. There was a big plate of chocolate brownies on the dining-room table, so he helped himself repeatedly. After he had eaten about nine squares, the host announced that they were marijuana brownies, and that one square would be enough for an adequate evening. Later that evening Mike was pretty far gone, especially after some time in the hot tub. As we were putting on our clothes after getting out of the hot tub, we heard Mike saying slowly out loud, "Now I'm putting on my left sock. . . . Now I'm putting on my left shoe. . . ." Steve laughed, and said, "Mike, we don't need a report of your activities." He replied slowly, "I know *you* don't, but *I do*!"

The proper place of words in our lives is to help us keep track of experiences, by labeling them and categorizing them. We can then use these labels like a filing system, to "call up" a particular kind of experience when it's useful to us. The words on a menu bring to mind the experience of the taste and texture of the food described, in order to help us make a decision about what foods to select. The words are not the food; they only point to the food. This seems like a simple and obvious fact—few people try to eat the menu—yet the world is full of people who can talk at great length *about* experience without ever having much of it.

There are two ways in which the words in this book can be useful to you. One is if they result in accessing experiences you have already had, and in demonstrating to you new and useful combinations, sequences, and ways to utilize those experiences. The other is to create new experiences by giving you specific directions which you can use to discover more about

ix

how your mind works. Like a road map, these directions will *only* be useful if you take the time to actually follow them, and use your senses to experience the actual territory that they lead you to.

We have presented these patterns as explicitly and systematically as we can, in order to make it easy for you to learn them. We have presented them in great detail, and warned you about all the mistakes we and others have made with them, to make it hard for you to use them inappropriately. Once you have taken the time to learn these methods thoroughly, you can become more flexible and artistic in utilizing them with clients, with confidence that your behavior will remain systematic and effective.

Many people accuse NLP of being technological, with the implication that it is cold and unfeeling. However, those same people are happy to use the technology of central heating to help their houses warm, instead of the smoky fire used by their ancestors. They also use antibiotics and immunization to keep their children healthy without thinking about the incredibly complex technology behind it.

Months of warm feelings won't help a child who is a poor speller, or release him from the resulting ridicule, feelings of failure and self-criticism; an hour or two of NLP technology can teach him how to spell and provide him with a sense of accomplishment and self-worth. All the empathy in the world won't help a phobic; a half-hour of NLP technology can release her from a life punctuated with terror. Holding the hand of a dying friend may ease his passing; appropriate medical technology may save his life.

Of course any technology can be misused by delivering it in a cold, unfeeling way. We have listened to nurses whose ''bedside manner'' must have been learned from a tape recording of Lucretia Borgia, and therapists who speak in the tonality of Adolph Hitler. This book is more technological than most, because we know that detailed technology gets results, and that the ''coldest'' technology can be delivered with humanity and respect.

We learned much of the material in this book directly from Richard Bandler in a small seminar in early 1984. In that seminar he taught us a number of specific patterns, most of which are included in this book. But more important, he demonstrated the tools of the trade: how to use fine distinctions, specific questions, and procedures for further exploration and discovery. Richard also often demonstrated without explaining, described events cryptically, or dropped tantalizing hints. Although this was often frustrating, it also whetted our curiosity and motivated us to explore further. Since then, we have been using the tools he taught us to follow up some of those tantalizing hints and develop specific patterns in sufficient detail that they can be more easily learned by others.

For over three years now we have been teaching this material in our Advanced Submodality Trainings. Much of this book has been edited from transcripts drawn from many different trainings. These segments have been woven together and presented as if they occurred in one training, both for your ease in reading, and to retain the conversational style and format of the live teaching. Other parts we have written without referring to tapes or transcripts. Most of the time we do not indicate which of us is speaking; after months of editing by both of us, we often don't know, and it doesn't matter anyway. We do identify ourselves in transcripts of demonstrations which are also available on videotape.

In many ways, this book is a continuation of Richard Bandler's book, *Using Your Brain—for a CHANGE*, which we edited two years ago. As we were writing this book we have presupposed that readers will have read *Using Your Brain*, and will have a background understanding of basic submodality patterns. If you don't have that background, we strongly recommend that you acquire it before reading this book, in order to get full value from the patterns in this book.

We also strongly recommend that you read the chapters in this book *in order*. Sequence, or syntax, of experience is a major organizing principle in NLP, and the sequence of chapters in this book has been carefully thought out. Many of the later chapters presuppose that you have already read and understood earlier chapters. If you read a later chapter without the background provided by earlier chapters and *Using Your Brain*, it will be more difficult for you to understand the material completely and thoroughly.

There is an old joke about the human brain being "the only self-maintaining all-purpose computer that can be created by unskilled labor." However, it's also a computer without an owner's manual. The patterns developed by NLP are essentially human "software"—ways to organize your experience that can be learned, a cultural/social resource, like all the other products of human creativity and inventiveness. The material we present here explores the mental patterning that makes us who we are, and provide tools that you can use to quickly change how you respond. This book joins over 30 NLP books that have been published since the first one was published by Richard Bandler and John Grinder in 1975. And this is only the beginning. . .

—Steve Andreas
—Connirae Andreas
September 1987

I

Timelines

Most of us have encountered people about whom we've thought, "Oh, she's living in the past," or "All he thinks about is the future; he never takes time to stop and smell the flowers," or "She only lives for today; she has no conception of where she's going." These qualities are determined by the ways people represent time internally. The ways people represent time—past, present, and future—provide the basis for their skills and limitations. Because of this it is impossible to fix some problems unless you change a person's way of representing time.

Some people talk about putting the past behind them," and that's exactly what they do. If you put the past behind you, you can't see it anymore, and it's gone. Others talk about having a dim future, and literally, the future on their timeline is dim. There are even people with no future at all.

Time is a very basic element in organizing our experience. Think what it would be like to experience a world without time. Without time there would also be no causality, no way to know what to do to satisfy needs, and no way to know when to do it. With *rare* exception, we all have *some* way of sorting experiences with respect to time.

In our explorations, we've discovered lots of interesting variations on how people represent time. After teaching the material on timelines to many different groups, we still have fun playing with it, and we think you will, too.

Elicitation Demonstration
Linda, may we elicit your timeline? (OK) First think of some simple behavior—like brushing your teeth, driving to work, doing the dishes, or

1

washing your face—that you did in the past, you do now, and you will do in the future.

Linda: I'll take brushing my teeth.

Fine. We'd like to have you think about a time when you brushed your teeth a long time ago—maybe five years ago.

Linda: I can't remember any particular time.

That's fine. You know that you brushed your teeth five years ago, right? So you can just pretend that you are remembering having done it five years ago.

Linda: OK.

Now I want you to think about having brushed your teeth a week ago. . . . (OK) Think about brushing your teeth now, . . . think about brushing your teeth a week from now, . . . and think about doing it five years from now. We'd like to have you get a sense that you are representing all these experiences at the same time, so that you can begin to notice what differences there are in the way you see this same event. . . . What lets you know that one is in the past and one is in the future? What differences in submodalities let you know one happened a long time ago, and one happened only a week ago?

Linda: That's easy. I lived in a different house five years ago, and I see myself in that house. That's how I know it was a long time ago.

This is a typical response. People tend to notice content differences first, but that's not what we want. We want the *process* differences that are coded in submodalities. Linda, what other differences do you notice between the long ago past and the recent past? If you need to, you can even pretend you lived in the same house five years ago, so you can notice only the submodality differences. Even if you *had* lived in the same house, you could probably tell the difference between five years ago and yesterday.

Linda: I don't think I could. To me it looks like five years ago (gesturing about two feet to her left) is just the same as a week ago (gesturing immediately to her left).

Those of you who were watching Linda's gestures know one way that she sorts time. She gestured to different locations.

Linda: Oh yeah! I guess I do see them in different places.

Great. Now notice how you see a week in the future, and five years in the future.

Linda: Those are in different places, too. They go off to my right. That's interesting. A week in the future is farther away from me than a week in the past. And five years into the future is really far away.

Excellent. That's the kind of thing we want you to notice. Check whether there are any other differences. Are your representations of the future different in any other way from your representations of the past?

Linda (pausing to check): The future looks less detailed.

That's a typical way of representing the future as less certain than the past. Now check the picture of five years ago and compare it to a week ago. Is it different in any way other than location? Check the size, brightness, and so on.

Linda: I guess the picture of five years ago is a little smaller. I hadn't noticed that before. . . . My future is like that, too. Five years in the future is smaller than one week in the future.

Exercise

I think this is enough of a demonstration to give you an idea of what we want you to do. Although you'll do this in groups of three, this is an exercise where you can all go inside right now as I give you directions, and begin to discover your own submodality codings for time. First think of some simple everyday behavior that you have done repeatedly in the past and will probably continue to do in the future. Pick something like going to work, brushing your teeth, doing the dishes, or taking a shower. Think about doing this behavior a long time ago, and then think about doing it in the recent past. Think about doing it in the present. Then imagine doing it in the immediate future, and finally, in the far future.

As you think of doing the same behavior at each point in time, keep the content the same, so that the only difference is *when* it's done. We want you to discover the submodality differences that are related to how you represent time. These differences will be much more apparent to you when you think about eating breakfast at different times *simultaneously*. When you imagine eating breakfast five years ago and five years in the future *at the same time*, what is the difference in the way you think of these two events? People typically represent time very differently when they access their experiences one at a time, sequentially. If you have trouble seeing all these pictures at the same time, use the "as if" frame: just pretend you can do it.

Do this individually and silently in your groups. After you have noticed as much as you can about your own way of sorting time, open your eyes and take turns describing your timeline to the other two in your group.

As each person describes her timeline, observe all the *nonverbal* indicators of time sorting. People are always providing nonverbal cues about their experience of time, just as Linda gestured to different locations for different times. This is particularly useful if someone's telling you,

"Oh, I don't sort for time. The far past (gesturing over shoulder) is the same as the present (gesturing a foot in front of face), and that's the same as the future (gesturing at arm's length); it's all the same." I am nonverbally demonstrating "my" timeline by gesturing behind me for far past, waving my hands directly in front of me for the present, and pushing my hands straight away from my body to indicate the future. Another person might say, "Yes, here's the past" (gesturing with hands about a foot apart), "here's the present" (moving both hands outward until they're about two feet apart), "and here's the future" (moving arms wide apart). By noticing these nonverbals you can get a good idea about how a person represents time. In the first example, *location* is a key submodality, and in the second one, *size* is more important, although location is also used. Nearly everyone uses location in space as one element of time-sorting.

After you have shared your representations of time, ask about anything that is unclear to you about the others' timelines, and then check for submodalities that were not mentioned: *detail, transparency, brightness, focus, color,* or anything else you might consider using as a way of coding time. Most people sort time with a combination of submodalities in addition to location.

You might also specifically notice whether past and future are different; people will often use a digital difference such as color vs. black-and-white or still picture vs. moving picture to distinguish between past and future. In these cases, there is probably also an analogue difference such as intensity of color or speed of movement that lets them know how far in the past or future something is. People usually have events arranged along a continuum of some kind. But check this out, because there will always be some people who have a totally different way of sorting time. Don't assume anything.

After you've characterized your own and your partners' timelines, we want you to experiment with temporarily adjusting your own timeline. Take some prominent feature of your own timeline, and change or reverse it in some way, and notice how that shifts your experience. For instance, Linda noticed that her future is more spread out than her past. She could try out seeing the past pictures more spread out, and the future pictures closer together, and notice what impact that has.

Let's say that size is a critical submodality for you: more recent experiences are bigger, and things that happened in the past are smaller. As an experiment, try reversing this, so that the more recent experiences are smaller, and events in the past are bigger. Does this change the relative importance of past and present events for you? How might someone with this kind of timeline function differently in the world? What are the advantages and disadvantages of each?

On my timeline the future starts about chest level and then goes up and to the right at about a 45-degree angle. So I might try tilting my future *down* at a 45-degree angle, and find out what impact that change has. How would this change the kind of person I am? When you experiment in this way, you may find that the changes you try feel weird or disconcerting. This is a strong indication that the timeline you have discovered is not arbitrary or just a result of our instructions, but is a significant way that you sort and respond to your experiences. Often your response simply results from the unfamiliarity of the change you are trying out. At other times, your response may indicate that you are trying to change something that is unecological to change, such as a basic element of your reality coding. Be sure to try out any changes cautiously and gently, and back off if you get strong ecological signals of disorientation.

Next you can experiment with trying out submodalities that others in your group use. Let's say that someone else's future is transparent. Try making your own future representations transparent, and discover how that change affects your response.

Finally, you can try on someone else's entire timeline. Find someone who sorts time very differently than you do. Take the timeline that seems the weirdest, the strangest, or the most bizarre, and try experiencing it to find out what happens. What would that timeline allow you to do that you can't do with your own? What could this make you really good at? And what limitations might it create? This exercise will be most interesting if you find a person who is quite different from you, because if you try on the timeline of someone fairly similar, you won't add very much to your choices.

Timelines are a major way of keeping track of reality for most people. By contrasting different ways of sorting time, you will learn more about the impact of your natural way of sorting time. When you try out different ways of representing time in contexts where you have problems or limitations, you can often discover interesting and useful applications.

Many of you will want to keep the way you already sort time. After you try out a different timeline, be sure to explicitly change it back. If you like a new time sort better, feel free to keep it, but be sure to do a careful ecology check first. Imagine taking this new time sort with you into the future. How does it work for you? You may want to have a new way of sorting time for some contexts in which you have been limited in the past, and keep your old way for other contexts in which you are already successful. Remember, NLP is about having more flexibility.

Exercise Summary
1. **Elicitation.** In trios, discover your own timeline and then share it with the others.
2. **Experimentation.**
   a. First adjust the submodalities that you already use, to discover how that changes your response.
   b. Then try out the submodalities that others use.
   c. Try out someone else's complete timeline.

* * * * *

Discussion: Location Sort and Relationship to Eye Accessing Cues
Did anyone *not* have a location sort for time? As we mentioned, the most common submodality that people use to sort time is location in space. This makes sense, when you think about it. The visual system is ideal for representing many events simultaneously. If you need to sequence a lot of representations, location is an excellent way to do it. If they were all in the same place, you could only see one at a time, and you'd have to code them by differences in brightness, color, size, or something like that.

For most people, the past is on their left, and the future is on their right, the way it was for Linda. For how many of you is that *not* the case?

Henry: My past is to my right, and my future to my left.

So yours is a reversal of the most common pattern. Are your eye accessing cues also reversed?

Henry: Yes.

The timeline is usually aligned with the person's accessing cues. People almost always have their past on the same side that they have visual memory, and their future is on the same side as visual construct. However, we have found a few people who have their timelines reversed with respect to their accessing cues. One man with this pattern complained a lot about the future seeming very "fixed," while his past seemed much more flexible. He said he could do the Change Personal History pattern (discussed in *Frogs into Princes*) very easily. You would expect this since his visual construct accessing was to the right, in the same general location as his past, so he could change past images easily. However, these changes wouldn't generalize into his future very well, because the future had the more fixed and detailed characteristics of visual memory. Most of us use constructed images to plan the future, an option that wasn't readily available to him. When he reversed his timeline, he had the sense that his future was more open and flexible.

Roxanne: I have normal accessing cues, but a reversed timeline.

You might find it interesting to try switching your timeline around so that it matches your eye accessing cues, and find out what impact that has.

Any time you play around with taking on a different timeline, there may be things that you're delighted with about the new timeline, especially in certain contexts. However, before adopting a different timeline, be sure to check for what your old one does that's valuable. Check all your major life contexts: work, play, family, etc. Even if you like the new one better for certain situations, you may want to keep the old one in some contexts.

Time Orientation

Let's talk a little bit more about past-, present-, and future-oriented people, and how their orientations relate to their time sorts. For example, one person that I worked with had the past right behind her, the present directly in front of her, and the future going out ahead. Now, what kind of person was she with respect to time? If you try on that timeline, what will your orientation be?

Al: I'm not sure. It's confusing.

Well, can you see the future?

Al: No, not really.

Not unless your pictures are transparent, and hers weren't! If the present is right in front of you and the immediate future is behind that, so you can't see it, what is your time orientation?

Sally: Present.

Right, and for her it was the *immediate* present. When she said "right now," she really meant *right* now—this split second! Five minutes from now would be in the future for her. She had a very narrow sense of the present.

Now try this out. What if your future goes off to your right at an angle, so you can see most of what's in each picture, and it gets bigger and brighter as it goes forward in time? The far future will be more important for you. You would tend to live for the far future, and respond less to the present and past.

If the near future or the present were bigger and brighter than the far future, you might experience difficulty with long-range planning or thinking about the consequences of your behavior, but be very good at planning immediate future events. Investigating your timeline can often give you some clues about how to change it in a useful way.

Carol: I started out being very present-oriented. My present was big, bright, and close, and both future and past were small and dim. We changed it so that I could keep all that wonderfulness of the present, but move some of that brightness into the next several weeks also, so that I'd respond more to the immediate future and get more done.

That sounds like a useful change. Here's another timeline you can all try out. One man had his past on a line straight in front of him. His future went way off to his right. You know the phrase, "My past flashed in front of my eyes?" This man lived that way all the time. What does that do to your experience? It certainly focuses your attention on the past. Depending upon whether your past was wonderful or horrible, you might like it or not, but you wouldn't pay much attention to the present or future. This is the kind of person for whom using the Change Personal History pattern will be very impactful, because he responds so strongly to representations of the past.

Carl: I've noticed that in certain circumstances I can focus a lot on the past. My past was right up here in front of me. So I just moved it over there to my left, and went, "Beep. Bang!" and slammed the door.

And how does that work for you?

Carl: Well, I don't know yet.

If you now take this new timeline into future situations, you can get a good idea of how it will work, and if any adjustments need to be made. The ideal is to have some flexibility with your timeline—to be able to move the past where you can see it when that's useful, and move it out of the way when you want to be more present- or future-oriented.

I think you are all getting the idea that *in general, whatever is right in front of you and noticeable—big and bright, colorful, etc.—will be most compelling and you will pay most attention to it.*

Useful Timelines

Fred: I'm interested in hearing about some useful timelines.

Well, the question is always "Useful for what purpose?" or Useful for whom?" You're getting a sense of what the possibilities are. Let me tell you some fairly standard ones. Most people have some kind of gentle, open curve, the way Linda has. The past is usually a line off to the left, the present right in front of you, and the future in a line to the right. Images may be stacked behind one another, but they're usually offset or arranged at an angle, so that part of each successive picture is visible.

Deciding whether a timeline is useful or not depends on what your personal outcomes are, and what's ecological for you. Saying "this is the *right* timeline" is like saying "this is the *right* way to be, and there are no other useful ways to live in the world." A person's timeline can make him unique. But if it gets him into trouble in certain situations, or if a different timeline would allow him to do things that he can't now do with his own, then it might be appropriate to explore alternatives, at least for specific contexts.

Timeline Spacing

It's often useful to find someone you think is very capable and skilled, investigate how she sorts time, and try it out. For example, people who are good long-range planners tend to have the future close in front of them rather than off to the side. We know a man who teaches business people long-range planning, and he's very good at it. He has both his five-year and his ten-year plans right there in front of him, very detailed, and quite close. Ten years is only about two feet away. That works fine for him, and he really likes it, but when I try it, the future seems to press in on me too much. I want the future a little bit farther away and less detailed, so that I have more room to move in the present.

What difference might it make in a person's life if his future timeline is really e-x-p-a-n-d-e-d instead of compressed, like that of the long-range planner I just mentioned? Try putting tomorrow halfway across the room, next week down the hall, and next month so far away on the horizon that it's barely visible. What might be the behavioral consequences of having such an "expanded" timeline?

Anne: I wouldn't be very motivated to do something that was way out there someplace! I'd feel as if I had a lot of time to kill before getting around to it.

Mike: How true! When I was writing my dissertation, finishing it was quite a way off in the future. There was lots of room to add other projects between the present and the completion date of my dissertation, so I kept taking on new jobs and putting off the dissertation. When I finally realized what was happening, I "reeled in" the deadline until it was so close to the present that there wasn't enough room to add anything in between. Any new projects had to get added on *after* the dissertation was done.

Nice! That's a good illustration of how compressing a timeline can help someone meet deadlines.

Lars: I think I need to do the opposite. My future is all bunched up close, and I always feel like the future is pressing in on me. When I spread it out a little more, I feel much more relaxed.

You look as if that it might lower your blood pressure 30 points. Let's check carefully for ecology, though. Imagine taking this new spread-out timeline with you through the next day, . . . and the next week. . . . Can you still get the things done you want to get done? Or are you *too* "laid back?"

Lars: No, not at all. In fact I think I can plan and schedule better. Before, my future was *so* bunched up that I couldn't really see it to plan very well.

That sounds good. We've also noticed that for some people, having a long-range future that is filled with big bright goals literally gives them "something to live for" and they're more apt to stay alive! One study on cancer patients found that survivors are apt to be future-oriented, whereas non-survivors are past-oriented.

Bob: I used to be much more future-oriented than I am now. In the past couple of years I've slowed down, and my future seems to be less clear than the way it was before. There are obviously advantages and disadvantages.

Absolutely. If you are too fixated on the future, you may not be taking care of things in the present. You may not notice that you're having a lousy time now, and that your family's having a lousy time, too. On the other hand, if all your attention is on having fun in the present, you won't notice the future consequences, and your future won't be as enjoyable as it could be. Depending on the consequences you ignore, it could be a lot shorter, too!

Differences Between Past and Future

Let me ask you another question: Did you notice any differences— especially digital differences—between past and future?

Bob: For me, past images are all seen out of my own eyes, and the future is dissociated images of myself.

Anne: My past and my future both have a foggy border around the pictures, but the color of the fog is grey for the past and silvery for the future.

Which do you like better, the grey or the silver?

Anne: The silver is much more appealing. That's why it's right in front of me.

Sally: I have something similar. My past is very dark, and the future has light around it; pictures of the far future are so small that all I can see is the brightness.

So you have a bright future!

Chris: Tom's timeline was very wierd to me.

Can we all try it, Tom?

Tom: Sure, I don't have a copyright.

Demonstrate how to do it.

Tom: My future has a peak in it. It goes off to the right, and the immediate future goes up in a peak, and then the more distant future drops back down, like the back side of a mountain, so I can't see it.

Have you explored changing this part of your timeline?

Tom: Not yet.

What happens if you take your future and straighten out that little peak, and make it all go in a straight line off to your right? How is that different?

Tom: I'm not sure.

When you level the future out so it's all in one line, are you more or less focused on the immediate future than when you had the peak?

Tom: I think I'm more oriented towards the far future when I can see that it's all in one line.

That would make sense. Having a peak in the immediate future focuses your attention on that portion of the timeline, and obscures what comes after it. When you can see the more distant future, you're more likely to respond to it.

Analogue Continuum vs. Digital Categories

That peak in Tom's timeline is an example of a sharp discontinuity in the timeline, in contrast to more gradual changes. Watch for that kind of discontinuity as a signal of a digital or categorical shift in how the person will respond. For example, instead of a smooth continuum, one man's timeline was like a string of bubbles or pop beads. Each bubble contained about 6 months of memories. Although the bubbles were sequenced in time, events *within* each bubble were randomly ordered. It would be easy to do change history with him, because you could easily install a new resource memory without any need to carefully fit the new memory in with whatever happened just before or after it.

Although most people use location as an analogue submodality, some people also make digital distinctions in location that are very important to know about. The person's nonverbal gestures often alert you to these categorical distinctions. Staccato gestures, or a hand flipping over like a coin in space, usually indicate categorical alternatives. Sometimes people will gesture with a slicing movement to draw a vertical or horizontal line indicating a definite demarcation between two locations. In contrast, moving the hand in a gradual way is usually a clear indication of an analogue continuum.

Changing Timelines

Woman: You keep describing changing the timeline by just visually rearranging it the way you want it. Is there anything else you need to do?

You always want to check very carefully for ecology, because timelines are very much tied into people's sense of what's real and what isn't. The past has already happened, so it's real, but the future hasn't, so it's *not* real. If you start changing those distinctions, you could seriously violate a person's reality. If the change you propose is fully ecological, it will happen easily.

We also frame any changes as temporary. "You can try this out; if you don't like it, or if it's not appropriate in some way, you can always go back to the way you did it before." To be really thorough, ask the person to imagine using the new timeline in all appropriate contexts. "What is it like to have this new timeline? Notice if it allows you to do what you want to do, and if it results in any problems or limitations." Changing timelines is a very major change—one that can impact all areas of your life. It's not something to undertake lightly. Before you change one, you want to be sure you know what you are doing. If a part of you is concerned that you'll be stuck with this new timeline, it will fight you all the way—and rightfully so.

If I want to install the new timeline permanently, I'll have the person think about where he wants to have new choices, and then I'll have him imagine taking the new timeline into several different future situations as a future-pace. Of course then I test to make sure that the new timeline has generalized by asking him to think of one or two other situations and discover how he responds in *those*. If he is satisfied with the results, our work is done. When you install a new timeline, you want to check both whether the person now sorts time in the new way, *and* if he can do what he wanted to be able to do.

Dawn: Are people disoriented at first? When I tried on someone else's timeline, I was very disoriented.

If by "disoriented," you mean that the new timeline seems unfamiliar, or takes a while to "settle in," that's a fairly common experience. If the feeling of disorientation is a feeling that the new timeline is not quite right for you, it may be because it *isn't* appropriate. Do you need something else to make it work for you? This is something to check out carefully if you're installing it, and not just trying it on.

Joe: I found it exhausting to take on other people's timelines. I actually got physically tired.

I notice that you use the phrase "to take on" a new timeline; it sounds as if you're dealing with an opponent or a burden. A number of people report feeling tired when they do this. It hasn't been my personal experience, and I think it's because rather than putting a lot of effort into it—by straining to force my pictures into new places—I just let the timeline do *me*. The images simply appear in new positions. Does that make sense? What did others experience as you tried different timelines?

Mark: I was working so hard at it that I began to feel some eye strain.

June: For me, trying a new timeline was more of an easy fantasy experience. I just let it happen, without trying to control it.

So you used something like the "as if" frame to experience a new timeline. Mark, you might want to try June's strategy. Pretend "as if" you already have the new timeline, but you don't necessarily have to see it clearly to know it's there. That may eliminate some of the strain on your eyes.

Adding a Future

Betty: I was amazed to find that I don't have a future! My timeline just stops about here (gestures about a foot to her right). People have always warned me about living too much for the present, and not thinking ahead. How can I add more of a future? I tried to add one, but it just doesn't make sense to me to be putting all those pictures out there on a line when I don't know what's going to happen.

That makes a lot of sense. This is an important ecological consideration. It sounds like you tried putting pictures out in your future that were as detailed and clear as those from your past. Think about what would happen if your future were very clear and detailed. You would see exactly who you were going to marry and how your marriage would go; you'd see clearly which job you would be working at, etc. If you get too detailed about the future, it's unlikely that the "real" future will be that way, and you will often be disappointed.

When you create a future for someone, you need to be sure you allow for the fact that you don't *know* what will happen. Many of you noticed that your future had some kind of indication of uncertainty. It might be foggy, or out of focus, or even transparent. Some people see different pathways in their future; they have more than one path to choose from, like water spraying out of a hose. One woman had future images in bubbles which floated around slowly and exchanged places to indicate uncertainty.

Here are several possibilities you can try, Betty. One way to see the future is as a *set* of possible pathways. Rather than a line, you can see *branches* going out, each showing you a possible unfolding future.

Another way to do it is to put your *values* or a general representation of your *outcomes*, into your future. You can put symbols in your future that represent the direction you want to go. Then you know what you want—what values are important to fulfill in your future—but you have lots of flexibility about exactly how to accomplish them.

Betty: That sounds good to me. . . .

So think about what's really important to you in your future. What do you want more of in your life? Do you want to do things that will allow you to learn . . . ? To become more and more capable . . . ? To have good relationships with those around you . . . ? Let your unconscious assist you in generating representations of what you are sure you want to have in the future. . . .

Betty: Yes, that works. . . . That's really different. . . . I'm putting things on a line out to my right, like the others in my group had.

And notice how this fits for you. If you take this timeline around with you, does it allow you to be more of who you want to be? Is there anything you still want to add or change?

Betty: I like it this way. I have the sense that I'll be different, though I'm not sure exactly how. I can think ahead better, and not just think about what appeals to me now. This seems more balanced. Thanks!

We've added future timelines for a number of people who had been without them. When you do this, you need to teach them how to keep their representation of the future as a possibility and not a fact. If you installed a detailed definite future, you would be setting the person up for disappointment, or a rigid pursuit of something very specific. If you do put in specifics, be sure you put in several pathways, so that the person isn't stuck with only one way, which might not work out.

Some people have a definite end to their timeline. Particularly if someone is older, you might want to check whether she is programming her own death, what the TA people call a "life script" or a "death script." That can be very useful to notice and consider changing.

Sally: I once tried to do a Swish with a woman who had been seriously injured in a car accident. Whenever I asked her to construct an attractive future, she had a very strong, negative reaction; she would get very upset and start crying. I discovered that she couldn't make any of her futures pleasant because she saw herself either dead or severely injured in all of them. Her past timeline zoomed around her left shoulder to a spot in front of her, but as it approached the present, the images all bunched together and didn't go anywhere. Her timeline just stopped. So I had her gradually extend her line into the future: "What will you do five minutes from now? How about next week?" Eventually she learned how to have a future again. It's amazing what a difference that made. There were so many things I tried that hadn't worked when she didn't have a future.

That's a nice example of how you can assist someone to chunk down the task of building a timeline so that she can master it in small steps. Notice, too, that you can't do a swish with a person who "has no future." Without a future, a swish is meaningless, and a lot of other things are meaningless, too.

Gary: Could you have used a Belief Change with that woman? She obviously believed that her future was over, she was dead.

Sally: That's interesting, because she'd been a thin person before the accident, but has gained weight since then. She has trouble losing it because she thinks that if she gets thin again, she might die.

So she may equate being thin with dying, and it might be appropriate to experiment with changing some of her beliefs. On the other hand, her weight gain could also be a result of her not having a future. When you're more present-oriented, the taste of food in the moment is more compelling. And there certainly isn't any motivation to lose weight if you expect to be dead soon anyway!

Creating a Timeline

In the previous cases, the person was missing the future *part* of his or her timeline. Once I encountered a woman who didn't even want a timeline *at all*! She refused to do the exercise. The people in her group were saying, "Just pretend; just do it, it'll be fun," but she didn't give in. "No, I don't want to! Do it without me!" When someone says, "No!" like that, it's time to be respectful of her and think about ecology rather than say, "This is the exercise. Follow the steps." She was absolutely right not to try on a timeline without making other arrangements first. When I sat down with her to gather more information, it turned out that her reluctance fit in perfectly with how she had been functioning in the seminar. She often got confused with respect to time and didn't sort things out the way other people did. She just had a big mish-mash of experiences that weren't sorted out by *when* they occurred. Her objection to neatly organizing everything into a timeline was that it would stifle her spontaneity, which she really valued. In this case, I helped her reframe "spontaneity," so that the spontaneous ability to have a timeline could allow her to be even *more* flexible—she could choose to have a timeline or not!

Mark: Are you saying that she really didn't have a timeline before that point?

I couldn't find one at all, and I tried! Even with people who aren't conscious of having one, I can usually find it. But I couldn't with this woman. Strangely enough, though, after the ecology issue of spontaneity was taken care of, she spontaneously developed a timeline! (laughter) She didn't have to construct it slowly and carefully, either; it just fell into place.

June: If this woman didn't have a timeline before then, how did she get to your workshop? She must have had some way to sort time if she had any concept at all of past, present and future. Did she, or was it really that bad?

I asked myself those same kinds of questions. She could get places, but she couldn't plan very well. She didn't have her life sorted out in that way. She was married, and her husband was good at sorting things out. Since she'd managed before getting married, she must have had *something* in her head keeping track of things! But it certainly wasn't well-formed in the way most people's are. At any rate, I presupposed that there was a part of her that went through life in a certain order, and would know where to put events on her new timeline. When I explained it in that way, she didn't have any trouble. Working with this woman was particularly interesting to me because it's very rare to encounter someone without a time sort, especially in seminars.

Pleasant/Unpleasant Experience Sort

Marge: For me, the content of an experience makes a difference in where it's stored on my timeline. If an incident is trivial or unpleasant, and I need to get rid of it, I put it behind me. But if it's something I want to remember or that I like, I put it up here (gestures toward upper left).

Several other people have that same kind of sorting principle. They put some things on a part of their timeline that they can't "see"—behind them somewhere—so those experiences don't bother them. On the other hand, things that are important go on parts of the timeline that are "visible"— usually to one side, or even in front.

Joe: I do that, too, but I wasn't aware of the unpleasant memories on the invisible part of the timeline until someone in my group asked me to put an experience behind me. I discovered that there was stuff back there because I had to move it around to make room!

I think you all recognize the advantages of separating resourceful experiences from unpleasant ones. However, what is one possible problem with that type of time-sorting?

Sam: You won't learn anything from the experiences you put behind you.

You *might* not learn from them. Jill puts the past behind her when she's through with it, but she also *first* extracts any useful learnings from her past and puts those into her future, *before* putting something behind her once and for all. That's very important to do before you "put the past behind you."

Sam: What about amnesia?

Well, I really don't know . . . uh . . . um . . . what were we talking about? (laughter)

Sam: Do people with amnesia put the past behind them?

No. Amnesia is different. If you put your past behind you, you don't think about it much, but it's still available to you. An amnesic seems to have no access to the past whatsoever—it's not *consciously* available in *any* location. It would be interesting to ask someone with amnesia where he thought the past would be, if he *could* remember it.

You can create amnesia by putting memories behind a barrier—a locked door, a black curtain, etc.—so that they are temporarily unavailable to the person. You can also create permanent amnesia by any form of complete disruption, such as taking a memory and sending it into a "black hole" or burning it to ashes (see Chapter 10), but in general we don't advise it. If you destroy a memory completely, that prevents you from *ever* making use of it.

All your experiences—both the good and the bad, the ones you have actually had, and the ones you can imagine—are valuable resources. If you limit your access to any of that, you impoverish yourself.

Let me give you an example of a method that helps people benefit from past unpleasant experiences without being bothered by them. A man in one of our seminars several years ago had been through a violent revolution in Latin America. After that he had been through some other horrors. This man claimed that he had no past timeline, and he wanted to have one. I tested this by asking him questions that presupposed a past time sort. Whenever I did that he got very confused. He'd "space out" for a moment, and then ask me what I had been talking about.

I had him take his entire past—much of which he had blanked out with good reason—and *unconsciously* dissociate from all of his unpleasant memories, and turn them into black and white images, so that they wouldn't bother him. That way he could still see his past memories and learn from them, but the feelings would be "over there." Then I had him take all of his pleasant memories and make sure that they were in color, so that he could respond to the positive memories fully. The result was that he was much less confused about the past because he had an effective and comfortable way of sorting his experiences.

Fred: Did you have him make the unpleasant memories into still pictures rather than movies?

I don't usually do that because you can store much more information in a movie of a past event than in a still picture, but it's certainly a possibility.

Fred: Was it easy for him to change his time-sorting?

Yes. Once I suggested what he might try, he seemed perfectly able to make the changes on his own. People's unconscious minds are very capable as long as you give explicit instructions. I asked his unconscious to sort through his entire history, and separate the pleasant experiences from the unpleasant ones.

After sorting memories, and dissociating from the unpleasant ones, you can go on to revise the unpleasant ones by adding in resources using change history, reframing, or some other pattern. When you have made them resourceful, the client can reassociate with them, and have them in color.

Al: You have mentioned the change history pattern a couple of times. Can you use timeline information when you do that?

Yes, in several ways. When you know someone's timeline, you can nonverbally pace him and make it much easier for him to go through the procedure. This is also true for many other techniques.

Knowing the timeline can also help the person generalize the change better. You can say, "Look back through the past and notice all the different times and places where you have responded in this *same* way." Then after you have changed one of these experiences—preferably a particularly intense or early one—you can presuppose that all the others will change *because they are the same.* "Since in all those different situations you used to respond in the same way, this new way of responding can also be appropriate and automatic whenever that kind of situation occurred in the past, as well as when it occurs in the future." You don't have to know about timelines to use that kind of language, but it helps. We sometimes tell people, "Watch as that change ripples through your timeline, changing all the events that happened before and after that situation."

The change history pattern is very useful. However, it only results in a new response to one content area, a particular kind of situation—even if you generalize it throughout your timeline. In contrast, when you change how your timeline is structured, you change the way a person processes *all* content. That's a much more profound kind of change, with a more far-reaching impact on behavior. This is the kind of change we're primarily discussing in this chapter.

For instance, one of our students had a client who had "bashful bladder"; he had trouble urinating if anyone else was around. He did change history on a lot of embarrassing incidents in this client's past, but it didn't help. It turned out that this client's past timeline had a big loop in it, like a rotating circular slide carousel, full of many humiliating experiences. As long as his timeline contained that loop, doing change history on those incidents didn't help, because the carousel would rotate to show yet another one in a literally endless succession. When he had the client straighten out the loop, the client could see that there was a finite number of incidents to deal with, and it became much easier.

Another client had just been through a crisis. Her husband had had an affair; he had renewed his commitment to her, and she had forgiven him, but she was still bothered and depressed. She said, "It's always this way; even when something is all worked out, I feel depressed for about six months, and then I'm OK." It turned out that her timeline for the past six months and the future six months overlapped, so she couldn't easily tell if something in that period—in this case, the affair—was in her past or future. Her timeline was in the shape of a "Y." The tail of the "Y" went straight in front of her, and on it she placed incidents from both the past six months and the future six months. After this period, her timeline branched out in a more typical fashion. When she separated her immediate past and future she felt better right away instead of having to wait six months.

Another woman had a timeline like an inverted horizontal "W." The immediate past angled out in front of her to her right, and then bent, so that the long-range past angled back behind her. Her immediate future angled out in front of her to her left, and then bent so that her long-range future angled back behind her. She said her timeline made sense out of her difficulty getting things done. She had trouble with being distracted by things that had just happened, or were about to happen.

When she changed her timeline to a more standard one with the future in a line to her *right*, and the past in a straight line to her *left*, she was very pleased with the results. Over the next few days she said she had an easier time concentrating on getting things done, because the immediate future and immediate past weren't right in front of her, distracting her. She also had an easier time planning for the future, because it didn't have the same disjointed quality that her previous bent future line had. She also found it easier to lose weight, because the future consequences of eating were more apparent to her.

Gary: I discovered that I have two different timelines. One is for historical events: the War of 1812, the Depression, that kind of thing. The other is for events from my personal past: childhood, high school, and so on.

We've occasionally discovered this with other people. It's fascinating to notice all the variations.

Richard: Our group noticed that some of us use different sorts for different types of things. For me, activities are on one timeline, but places are on another.

So you have timelines organized differently according to content. Now *that's* flexibility!

Gary: Do people ever have time circles or something else besides lines?

We've found mostly lines. I did find one woman with a time circle, with her future circling around to her right, and her past circling around to her left. The distant past and distant future were directly behind her. She had the sense that her past and future joined behind her, but she wasn't sure exactly how.

One man had a very detailed "time helix." At a small chunk level, each cycle of the helix made up a week. Many of these small circles together curved around in a larger helix, like a curved spring, to make up a year. The years curved around in an even larger helix to make a century. This man remembers things, in minute detail—he was always very good at history.

We haven't checked, but we suspect that in Eastern cultures you might find more circles or cycles. There are lots of cyclical metaphors in Eastern religion: the wheel of life, the cycle of death and rebirth, etc.

Other Examples of Timelines

A computer engineer had his past behind him and his future appeared as a series of *transparent* color slides that went straight out in front of him. When he wanted to see into the future, he would make the ones in the immediate future very big and enlarged, so that he could see *through* them into the next one. If he wanted to see farther, he'd enlarge those and see through those to the next, and so on. His immediate future literally colored the more distant future. Try that one out if you want an altered state. That's one of the more unusual timelines we've encountered.

Ann: I just tried that timeline with something really neat from my past. With that transparent timeline, when I went back to a resourceful time, that resource changed the immediate future, and the immediate future colored the farther future, and made that more resourceful, too.

That is a very useful thing to do whenever you use the change history pattern, the fast phobia cure, or any other NLP pattern to alter a past representation. After you have changed a particular memory from a particular location on the timeline, you can say, "That old experience was like a filter that made you respond to later events in a particular way, coloring them in ways you couldn't ignore or change. Now the same will be true of this new way of experiencing that past event. As you place this memory back in its place on your timeline, I want you to notice how it will alter and recolor all the events between then and now, in a 'domino' effect, so that you will *enjoy* the benefits of that change *now,* as well as at all intermediate times in the past." That's a very specific instruction to generalize the benefits of a change.

One woman's future angled out *behind* her to her *left* and her past angled out *behind* her to her *right*. She was the point of a "V" which diverged behind her. Guess what she was.

Sally: The figurehead of a ship? (laughter)

Several people: Present-oriented!

Very present-oriented. At first she wasn't aware of where her timeline was at all, but I saw where her arms gestured when I asked about the past or future. Once she became aware of her timeline, she said it made sense out of the way she functioned. She was very present-oriented, and other people complained because she didn't plan well enough for the future. Luckily her husband was a *very* good planner. I suggested that the group help her experiment with other timelines to find out if something else would work better for her. It wouldn't be wise to simply swing her past and future lines around in front of her, because her accessing cues were normal so she would still be trying to access the future with remembered pictures and the past with constructed pictures. Her group tried to get her to think about time the way most people do, and she couldn't do it. She finally told them, "You know, I feel as though I'm all turned around." So they had her actually turn around physically, leaving her timeline in space where it was. She quickly spun around before her timeline could move. That may sound a bit bizarre, but it worked! Suddenly she had a lot more "time on her hands,'' and she liked being able to more easily think about the past and plan for the future.

Another person with regular accessing cues had her past in a line going down and to her right. When she thought about her past, guess which representational system she tended to access strongly?

Audience: Kinesthetic! Feelings!

Right. She thought of unpleasant past experiences "with great feeling." That's how she talked about it. She didn't like that too well, so she tended to focus on the future instead. She decided to move her past up and to her left, where most people put theirs. After doing this, she could think about the past without the intense bad feelings. I encouraged her to keep her old way of sorting time if she wanted to think about *pleasant* past experiences.

One man's past was on a line straight in front of him, slightly to his right. It angled up, so he could see it all. His present was directly in front of him, and his future was in a slot above and a bit behind his head. He said to me, "I'm pretty good at taking the future, pulling it down, stepping into it, and manifesting it, but I would like to know if there's a way that I could set up my timeline so that I could manifest the future even faster." This is someone for whom the new behavior generator pattern is a snap!

Knowing that his future is up above his head, what do you think about his request? Remember, he wants to be able to pull down his future images and step into them faster than he already does. Is that an ecological request?

Chris: It's fairly ecological, because when he thinks of something in the future, he tries it on. That way he can get a kinesthetic representation of that possibility. If he doesn't like it, he can step out of the picture, and choose to go a different route.

It would be fine *if* he did that. However, he didn't ask to be able to *decide* better. He wanted to "manifest the future faster." He wanted to be able to step in and go for it. He didn't mention anything about having the flexibility to step out of a future he doesn't want. You probably have that ability, Chris, but I got no indication that *he* had it. He'd simply get the next image in line, pull it down, and step into it! Think about that for a moment. He couldn't see his future very clearly anyway—the pictures were up over his head—so he could hardly know the details of what was in them. And he wanted to do it faster!

As we did more exploring, it turned out that he had two locations for storing past events: his unpleasant past went out to his left, and he didn't look at it. Only his "good" past was on the line right in front of him. So the only past experiences that he looked at were the ones in which he was successful. How do you think that affected him?

Bob: He would only repeat what had worked in the past.

June: He wouldn't learn from his mistakes.

Sally: He was a risk-taker.

Right! Since he only accessed how things had worked, not how they had fallen apart, he took a lot of risks but didn't learn much from his mistakes. He could make these wonderfully successful futures and just step into them, so he came across as "Mister Confidence." He would go for things with congruence, but it was a congruence that lacked depth. He didn't fully utilize the times things didn't work out—the counter-examples, and the exceptions—all of which *could* have helped him achieve his goals in a realistic way. We heard later that he got involved in a big business venture and went bankrupt.

Bob: I come from an athletic background, and it seems to me that in athletics that kind of confidence could really be useful.

Yes, that's a good point. *When*, exactly, would it be useful for you to only access success examples and step into them?

Man: When you're skiing down through the slalom poles.

Yes. When you're actually committed to going down the hill, you want to access doing it *right*, not all the times you hit the poles. So this man had a skill many people could use. However, *ahead of time*, when you're deciding, "Do I want to go down that slope?" it's a lot better to think about whether or not you might get hurt if you do.

When to Use Timeline Adjustments

Man: When would you want to adjust someone's timeline? If you were working with someone, what would let you know that it might be appropriate?

If a person isn't functioning the way she wants to, and I can't put my finger on why, I start wondering if it's caused by something about the timeline or some other basic structure. If the problem is a simple stimulus-response type of thing, you can use one of the standard anchoring or reframing patterns (described in *Frogs into Princes*), or the swish (described in *Using Your Brain—for a CHANGE*). When none of the standard patterns seem to work, that's another indication.

In some situations there are obvious indications to change time sorting. If someone is overly past-oriented—especially if she's preoccupied with a lot of unpleasant past experiences—it may be useful to help her move the past farther out of her visual field, in addition to changing specific events. Some people have the past on a line immediately in front of them, and this usually distracts them from going forward in life. On the other hand, some people are so future-oriented that they can't enjoy the present, or use the past as a resource. Others complain about being too impulsive and aren't capable of planning for the future. Whenever people complain of overeating, or abusing drugs, that's a strong indication of someone being very present-oriented. Some people will come right out and tell you that they have no future. That's about as close as we can get to telling you when this approach might be useful. We invite you to explore.

Some of you have asked about the ethics of changing people's timelines, or of creating them for people who don't seem to have them. Since your timeline underlies all your skills and limitations, changing the way you sort time can lead to some new and useful abilities, *or* it can eliminate them. If your outcome is to help someone solve a certain difficulty, the most ethical thing for you to do may be to change his timeline. Like any other change you help someone make, it's ethical as long as you're installing something that is ecological, and that will make a useful difference to him.

If your outcome is only to find out how a person sorts time so that you can learn from him, you simply gather information as cleanly as possible. When I'm doing this, one way I keep from installing anything is to let him lead me with his verbal and nonverbal cues. If I do make suggestions that could lead the person, I always make two or three, which allows him to choose: "How can you tell it's now as opposed to yesterday? Is the picture bigger? Is it closer? Is it in a different location?" If you give him only one option—"Is the picture closer? Is that how you can tell?"—it's too easy for him to follow your lead without checking, and you many unwittingly install a change that isn't useful.

Although you can come up with all sorts of ideas about a person's timeline and how it might work, it's most useful to invite that person to make his own discoveries without imposing your theories on him. Remember, he is always the expert, and you want to explore *his* reality with respect, not bulldoze him with your own. When you approach it with this frame of mind, you can often learn something totally new and fascinating, something very useful to you and to your other clients that otherwise might never occur to you. This attitude of fascinated exploration is a lot of what NLP is about—and it also makes your work much easier and more fun.

II

Utilizing Time

When we describe events, we use verbs and verb tenses to indicate their location in time. Like so much of language, we take verb tenses for granted, and usually don't realize the impact they have. Notice what you experience as you read the following sentence:

"I'd like you to look forward with anticipation to what you're doing now, reminiscing about what you will have accomplished at the conclusion of your life, while noticing what you are experiencing on your fifth birthday."

If that sentence disorients you or gives you a slight headache, it's because it uses words that keep reorienting you in time, in ways that are contradictory. Simplified, it says: "Look forward (from the past) to what you are doing now in the present, and back at the future (from the more distant future) as you notice where you *are* in the distant past." Often the impact of language on experience only becomes apparent when we encounter a violation of the usual rules.

Knowing how to use verb tenses can be a powerful aid to your communication. If you don't know what you are doing, it's easy to use verb tenses accidentally to *install* a problem on someone's future timeline by presupposition. When attempting to make changes, you can work against yourself by using inappropriate verb tenses. We'd like to explore how you can use verb tenses systematically to have a useful impact.

First let's examine the different specific verb tenses in English. Notice your internal experience as you say each of the following sentences to yourself. First are the simple verb tenses: "I talked to her" (past). "I talk to her" (present). "I will talk to her" (future). When saying "I talked to her," most people are associated in the present, and see themselves (dissociated) talking to someone on their past timeline. When saying, "I talk to her," most people are associated into the activity and visualizing only the other person listening. When saying, "I will talk to her," people usually are associated in the present, and see themselves (dissociated) talking to someone on their future timeline.

Notice how your experience changes when you use the -ing verb form (progressive tense) to express the same three time frames: "I was talking to her." "I am talking to her." "I will be talking to her." For most people, using the -ing turns their pictures into movies. "Talk*ing*," "runn*ing*," "do*ing*," "learn*ing*," etc. are *ongoing activities* that can't be adequately represented with a still picture. Often the pictures become larger or closer as well, and some people associate into the picture, even if they are speaking of the past or the future. Try this out yourself. Say, "I *ran* to the store." and then, "I *was running* to the store." Do you have a movie for the second sentence (or a longer movie)? Are you either associating into the second sentence, or finding your picture getting closer or larger?

Try a simple experiment to demonstrate the impact of tense shifts. First think of a simple problem or limitation you have, and notice how you represent it. . . .

Next read each of the sentences below, substituting your internal representation for the word "problem." Each time, pause to notice how your representation shifts. If you don't immediately detect a change, go back and forth quickly between two adjacent sentences to make the contrast more obvious, or alternate between two other sentences that are farther apart to accentuate the difference between the two.

I will have this problem.
I have this problem.
I had this problem.

I will be having this problem.
I am having this problem.
I was having this problem.

Now take the time to think of an appropriate resource state, . . . and notice how you represent it. . . . Notice how the submodalities of your internal representation of this resource shift when you shift verb tense as indicated below.

I had this resource.
I have this resource.
I will have this resource.

I was having this resource.
I am having this resource.
I will be having this resource.

If you want someone to dissociate from a past problem, it will be helpful to use the simple past tense, "You had a problem." If you want someone to associate more fully into a past resource, use the -ing form, "You were experienc*ing* this resource." This will be more useful than the simple past tense as a first step toward leading him into a full associated present experience of the resource.

The perfect tenses are even more interesting to explore. "I had talked to her" (past perfect) refers to a past event which ended *before* another past event. Three points in time are implicit in this sentence: "I" am associated in the present, thinking about an event in the distant past, which took place *prior to* another event in the more recent past. Generally the two past events are dissociated. The event described is not only located in the past; it is followed by an unspecified later event which exists *between* the speaker and the described past event. This increases the dissociation between the speaker and the past event.

You can use this information to help someone dissociate from a problem and place it in their distant past while you're "just gathering information." "So you're telling me that you *got* jealous every time your wife spoke to another man? Is that what you *had done*?" If that's too big a jump for the client, you can use more gradual verb shifts to lead up to it, "Is that what you have been doing? So that's what you had been doing." You will probably need to do more to resolve the problem completely, but you can use verb tenses carefully to support your work.

This has a very different impact than saying, "So when is it that you *get* jealous? Is it that you *will get* jealous every time your wife speaks to another man?" Those sentences actually program the person to keep responding with jealousy in the future!

"I have talked to her" (present perfect) refers to a past event which may or may not continue into the present. This ambiguity can be used as an intermediate step when you want to shift an experience from present to past, or the reverse. "So you *have had* this problem . . ." suggests that the future may be different, but since it is ambiguous, you won't violate rapport by saying this. "So until now, you *have felt* incompetent when your children haven't done what you *had asked* them to do."

"I will have talked to her" (future perfect) is even more interesting. It refers to a future time *after* another future event. Its effect is to reorient the speaker into the distant future. From this viewpoint the speaker looks back to a "past" event which has actually not yet occurred at the moment the speaker is talking. "So after you have solved this problem, *will* you *have noticed* the positive results that you *got* from changing?" For many people, putting something in the past gives it a sense of reality. You can use this verb form to put a change in the past, with respect to a future time, so that the change begins to seem "real."

There are three other verb forms that link two time frames in interesting ways.

"Having talked to her . . ." ("having" plus past participle) presupposes an event completed before another event. "Having made that change, what do you think your attention will be focused on next?"

"I hope to talk to her" (present plus infinitive). The event (talk) follows a present event (hope), expressed as an intention (outcome). "You'd like to feel resourceful in that situation."

"I was glad *to have talked* to her" (past plus perfect infinitive). A presupposed event (talk) precedes an evaluation (glad), which is itself in the past. As with "had talked," there is a past event between the speaker and the described event, amplifying the dissociation. "Were you concerned to *have had* that problem?"

All NLP involves accessing and resequencing experiences in time. One very broad general formulation of change work is that you start with a problem state, and then identify and access an appropriate resource state. Finally you install the resource state so that it's triggered in response to the same cues that previously had been the triggers for the problem state. You can accomplish this completely behaviorally by nonverbally eliciting and sequencing experiences in real time, as an animal trainer does. But if you do use words, you will find yourself using verb tenses to resequence events in internal subjective time. For example, "When you notice those cues that used to result in your feeling bad, you can experience these satisfying feelings instead."

Here is an example of Richard Bandler doing "torpedo therapy" using verb tense shifts. Before reading it, think of a personal change you'd like to make, and use this change as the content referred to.

"What will it be like when you have made those changes . . . *now* . . .

in the future . . . as you look back and see what it was like to ha
that problem . . . as you think about it *now*, here, sitting in this room?''

Another way to describe what Richard did in that sentence is that in order to solve a present problem or limitation, you can go through the following steps.

1. If I have a problem I can't solve, I am associated into the problem state, in the present. I may have no awareness of the desired state.

2. The first step toward change is for me to think of the desired state, *dissociated*, as a possibility in the *future*. So I *see myself* acting resourcefully in the future.

3. Next I dissociate from the present problem state, and associate into the future resourceful self. Now I am *in the future, with resources.*

4. From this future vantage point, I can see the old problem behavior in the completed past.

5. Now I can collapse the future "now" with the present "now" so that I experience the resources in the present, and the problem as *over* in the past.

Of course, just saying Richard's words won't automatically change someone; they have to be delivered with appropriate timing, hypnotic intonation and tonal shifts, within a context of rapport and responsiveness, with feedback that indicates that the person is actually accessing the appropriate experiences, etc. Appropriate verb tense shifts can be a powerful ally in all your change work, and inappropriate verb shifts can mess up what otherwise would have been an effective piece of work.

Here is a variation of the same sequence, again from Richard Bandler's "torpedo therapy." Read it slowly enough to notice the impact on your experience.

"If you could make this change for yourself . . . so that you could *stop* that old behavior you used to do . . . having already made that change, and see yourself as you are . . . now . . . do you like what you see?

When you know someone's timeline, you can amplify this process by using congruent hand gestures to help access different time frames and shift the client's orientation in time.

We have emphasized how you can use time words to shift someone's experience. You can also gather valuable information from clients or friends by *listening* to their verb tenses. If your client "spontaneously" starts talking about his problem in the *past tense*, this lets you know the problem has shifted into the past. For example, "I'm amazed at how much trouble that *caused* me" is very different from "I'm amazed at how much trouble this *causes* me." Verb tense is an additional way to test your work. If your client continues to speak of the problem in the present and future, you may not be done. But if the client speaks of the problem in past tense, that's a good indication that you have succeeded. To be sure, test behaviorally or with a detailed future-pace.

Cause-Effects

Everyone uses cause-effect understandings to comprehend and predict events. (Whether or not this is philosophically sound is a completely separate issue that thinkers have been arguing about for years.) The cause must always exist earlier in time than the effect. Even when the cause is an understanding of a probable future consequence, that *understanding* has to occur at an earlier time than any effects caused by it. Because of this, cause-effects depend absolutely upon an orderly sense of time. If we weren't able to arrange events in a sequence, we would not be able to make cause-effect connections. Most of our understandings would dissolve into chaos, as happens in some of the more disorganized forms of mental illness.

People who feel powerful perceive themselves as *causes* with choices about changing their situation, and this motivates them to take action. In contrast, people who feel helpless perceive themselves as *effects*, rather than causes. Besides the typical response of depression—and the lack of motivation, substance abuse, and other problems that depression often leads to— there are extensive well-documented physiological effects, including suppression of the immune system, and shorter life span. In an unpublished preliminary study of survival of stage four melanoma (skin cancer) patients,* the ones who believed that their behavior could have an effect on the progress of the cancer lived longer. In contrast, those who believed that the cancer had "just happened to them" and that there was nothing they could do to alter the course of the disease died quickly.

Since cause-effect beliefs are so vitally important to maintaining a coherent internal world, it makes sense to examine how we represent them. Think of some simple cause-effect relationship that *you* believe to be true, such as "rain makes the grass grow," or "a loving childhood produces well-balanced adults." Then notice the submodalities you use to represent this cause-effect. . . .

---

*Dr. Martin Jerry, Tom Baker Cancer Centre, 1331 29 St. NW, Calgary Alberta, T2N 4N2 Canada.

One way to do it is with a complete and detailed movie (associated or dissociated) of the events leading from cause to effect. Or you can shorten this complete movie into a film strip; although it has much less fine detail, the cause-effect relationship probably stands out more clearly in the strip. You can also use a simpler diagram, or two still pictures joined by an arrow, etc.

Since these cause-effect representations are so basic to maintaining a coherent world, they are often difficult to change. If you try to *eliminate* a limiting cause-effect belief such as "My abusive childhood makes it impossible for me to feel safe in a close relationship," you are literally attacking part of the person's way of understanding. It is typically much easier to create a *new* cause-effect that uses the same evidence in a new way to overshadow or reverse the presuppositions of the limiting one. For instance, you can say, "You have had a miserable childhood, which you can recall in minute detail. You know from personal experience the kind of things that crazy mixed-up people will do, and you know well the warning signals that indicate when this is about to happen." This is all a complete pace of the person's experience. Then you begin to lead her in a new direction. "Others who had a happy childhood never had the opportunity to learn all that. They may *feel* safe in a close relationship, but they're just living in a fool's paradise that could be shattered at any time. They are like small children walking happily into the African jungle. Because you *know* what can happen and can be on the lookout for it, you can know far better when you are truly safe. Because of your childhood you can actually be much safer than others who just *feel* safe because they don't know any better." Changing cause-effects is a big part of what is called "Meaning Reframing." (For more about this, read *Reframing* by Bandler and Grinder.)

Time Presuppositions

For years NLP practitioners have been using presuppositions. Submodalities helps you understand *how* they work. Of the 24 syntactic forms for complex presuppositions, nine of them depend on time, and these are among the ones typically used most often in hypnotic inductions. The most frequently used category, called "Subordinate Clauses of Time" includes such words as *before, after, during, as, since, when, prior, while*, etc. These words create presupposed sequences or linkages (in contrast to explicit conscious cause-effects) between experiences in time.

Try the following experiment. First make a representation of eating dinner at a restaurant, . . . and then make a representation of "discussing a proposal." . . . Now notice your experience of the following sentence: "Let's eat dinner at a restaurant before discussing a proposal." . . . Notice how the two representations become smoothly linked together in your mind. Unless you are adept at identifying presuppositions, this process occurs unconsciously. (Try reading that sentence *without* linking those two representations.) Now try a slightly different sentence: "Before we discuss a proposal, let's eat dinner at a restaurant." In this case, the first representation you make "discussing a proposal" moves aside to your less-detailed peripheral vision, in order to make room for "eating dinner at restaurant." In each case the result is the same; the presupposed representation becomes linked to the other, more conscious one. The process of getting there is slightly different, due to the different order of the two sentences.

Now try using the word "as." Notice how you represent the sentence, "As we discuss the proposal, let's eat dinner at a restaurant." . . . Now try the reversed sentence: "Let's eat dinner at a restaurant as we discuss the proposal." . . . With both of these sentences, the two representations blend together into the same time-frame. Most people find the first sentence easier to process, because the very first word, "as," alerts you that you will be putting two representations together. The second sentence requires you to go back and change the representation you started with after it's already formed.

If you go on to experiment with the other time words listed above, you can discover for yourself how they alter your submodalities to link representations together in your mind.

In the same way, you can discover the impact of the other eight syntactic presuppositional forms that utilize time, which are listed below (Reprinted from the Appendix of *Patterns of the Hypnotic Techniques of Milton H. Erickson, M.D. Vol. I* by Richard Bandler and John Grinder, pp. 257-261). The second sentence in parentheses is presupposed in the previous sentence in quotes.

1. Complex Adjectives: *new, old, former, present, previous.* "If Frodo wears his old ring, I'll be blown away." (Frodo has a new ring.)

2. Ordinal Numerals: *first, second, third, forth, etc.* "If you can find a third clue in this letter, I'll make you a mosquito pie." (There are two clues already found.)

3. Repetitive Cue Words: *too, also, either, again, back, another.* "If she tells me that again, I'll kiss her." (She has told me that before.)

4. Repetitive Verbs and Adverbs: verbs and adverbs beginning with *re-: repeatedly, return, restore, retell, replace, renew.* "If he returns before I leave, I want to talk to him." (He has been here before.)

5. Change-of-Place Verbs: *come, go, leave, arrive, depart, enter.* "If Sam has left home, he is lost." (Sam has been at home.)

6. Change-of-Time Verbs and Adverbs: *begin, end, stop, start, continue, proceed, already, yet, still, anymore.* "My bet is that Harry will continue to smile." (Harry has been smiling.)

7. Change-of-State Verbs: *change, transform, turn into, become.* "If Mae turns into a hippie, I'll be surprised." (Mae is not now a hippie.)

8. Counterfactual Conditional Clauses. Verbs having subjunctive tense. "If you had listened to me and your father, you wouldn't be in the wonderful position you're in now." (You didn't listen to me and your father.)

Notice how many of these sample sentences use the "if-then" cause-effect structure. You can create sentences using these syntactic forms without using "if-then," but they will still contain cause-effects.

Compelling Futures

One of the unique things about human beings is that we are able to make representations of the future, and that these future representations are often motivating; they can compel us to do things now, in order to create the kind of future we want to have. Take a little time now to do a short exercise in which you discover the submodalities that make an imagined future event compelling to you.

Exercise

1. Compelling future. Think of a future consequence (X) that compels your present behavior. This could be an unpleasant consequence—the thought of a car accident gets you to put on seat belts regularly—or it could be a pleasant consequence—you take care of your yard because you think of being able to enjoy it in the summertime.

2. Uncompelling future. Think of a future consequence (Y) of the *same* type (pleasant or unpleasant) that *doesn't* compel your present behavior, and you believe it would be valuable if it did. Be *sure* that (Y) is the same kind of consequence that you chose in the previous step. If (X) is an unpleasant consequence, then (Y) should also be an unpleasant consequence—for instance, the thought of losing all your teeth to gum disease *doesn't* get you to floss your teeth. If (X) is a pleasant consequence, then (Y) should also be a pleasant consequence: you know that your car will look nice if you clean it regularly, but you never actually get around to doing it.

3. Contrastive analysis. Compare these two representations to determine the submodality differences. Test each difference to discover which submodality shifts can be used to make (Y) compelling.

4. Ecology check. Does any part of you have any objection to your transforming (Y) into a consequence that *will* compel your behavior in the present, so as to reach the desirable consequence or avoid the undesirable consequence? Deal with any objections or concerns respectfully and completely before proceeding.

5. Mapping across. Use the submodality differences you identified to transform (Y) into a representation that compels your behavior in the present.

6. Test. Does this future representation now motivate your present behavior?

Reality Constraints

This is another simple and direct application of the principles of contrastive analysis of submodality differences and mapping across. As usual, representations of consequences that are bigger, brighter, closer, more colorful, etc. typically get a stronger response from you, and are more likely to compel your behavior.

However, in order to be compelling, a consequence also has to be *real* and *believable*. If you review the submodality differences you just found, there are some that have to do with how you code reality. These help you to distinguish between a consequence that you consider very unlikely and one that you really believe will happen. One participant thought of the unpleasant consequences of smoking by seeing a *cartoon* of what could happen to a smoker. He saw Mickey Mouse getting black lungs. Needless to say, this did *not* compel his behavior. The future was not represented in such a way that the results of smoking seemed real to him.

Now try a little experiment. Think of something (Z) that you *could* do, but it's unlikely that you ever actually would do—for example, sitting in the bathtub with your clothes on—and notice how you represent this.

Now say to yourself, "I *could* do Z." ("I *could* sit in the bathtub with my clothes on"). . . .

Then say, "I *can* do Z" ("I *can* sit in the bathtub with my clothes on"), and notice what changes. . . .

Next say with conviction, "I *will* do Z" ("I *will* sit in the bathtub with my clothes on") and again notice what changes. . . .

A typical response is that "I *could* do Z" is located wherever you freely consider possibilities, no matter how unlikely; it is *not* on your timeline. "I *can* do Z" usually moves toward your future timeline, and "I *will* do Z" is actually on your future timeline. Of course, it won't *stay* on your timeline if it's not a congruent and ecological decision.

One characteristic of a positive compelling future representation is that it is located on your timeline. A representation that isn't on your timeline generally won't be compelling, no matter how big and bright it is. Your brain may think "It's interesting, but it doesn't apply to *my* life." A compelling future representation needs to have the same submodality characteristics as those that are typical of your believable future representations. If it differs significantly from your other future representations, it may not seem believable to you, and it won't compel your behavior. Often future consequences don't compel behavior because they are *so* extreme that they are unbelievable caricatures.

Many people automatically represent a future consequence as more real if they have personally experienced that consequence at some time in the past. Small children often don't represent future consequences as real until they've actually experienced them in the real world. We *told* our little boys about hot stoves, but it wasn't until they reached out and *felt* the stove that they made a compelling and dependable representation of something to avoid.

Direct personal experience is a powerful teacher, even for adults. Many people stop smoking instantly (and easily) after a heart attack or a stroke provides compelling personal evidence of the consequences. In a recent controlled study, wife-abuse complaints were randomly assigned to two groups. In one group the abusive husbands were arrested and jailed, while in the other group they were only warned. Of those warned, about 70% repeated their abuse. Of those arrested, only about 30% repeated their abuse, and many of these spontaneously reported that *they thought their first arrest was an unlucky accident that wasn't likely to happen again in the future*. The first arrest wasn't enough to build a compelling future for them.

As you get older you have more of an experiential base from which to construct a compelling future consequence that you haven't actually experienced. Most people don't have to be hit by a truck to make a compelling image that prevents them from stepping in front of one. This works well as long as the situation is not too far beyond what you have experienced. Even someone who has experienced full-scale war can't represent an all-out nuclear exchange in which the destruction of *all* of World War II would occur every *minute* for most of a day. Since we can't represent such futures in a compelling way, they unfortunately don't have much impact on our planning.

In discussing compelling futures we have *presupposed* that the person perceives a cause-effect relationship between present behavior and future consequences. Sometimes a person perceives the future consequences vividly and believably, but he doesn't believe that there is anything he can do to influence these consequences. In this case building a compelling future would be redundant. Instead you need to create subjectively real cause-effect beliefs that connect present actions to future consequences.

When someone perceives a cause-effect relation between a behavior and a pleasant future consequence, he can simply decide what, where, and when the behavior needs to be done, and future-pace those behaviors.

However, when someone perceives a cause-effect relation between a present behavior and an *un*pleasant future consequence, it is not quite so simple. It would *not* be useful to simply future-pace this behavior and its undesirable consequences! When an unpleasant future consequence compels a person to alter her behavior, it's because it triggers a useful polarity process. Typically the person responds by literally saying "No," or "I don't want that," and then goes on to develop an alternative behavior, with alternative pleasant consequences. It's this alternative *desirable behavior and consequences* that go on the person's timeline in the future.

If you select an unpleasant consequence that already motivates you to do something *useful*, and then *map across*, these other elements will usualy fall into place automatically. When you make the new unpleasant consequence the same as the old one, since it already has the other necessary elements, it will motivate you to do something useful.

For future planning you need a compelling future to motivate you, cause-effects to know what to do, and future-pacing to actually program these behaviors. If any of these steps is missing, you will not be able to use time to forecast and respond to events.

III

The Swish Pattern

In the two years since we edited Richard Bandler's book *Using Your Brain—for a CHANGE*, we have accumulated a lot more experience with the fine points that make this pattern work. In this chapter we describe a number of detailed guidelines for creating an effective swish in any representational system, and provide unique case examples of making the swish work with clients. We are assuming that you have read the chapter about the swish in *Brain*. Our videotape "The Swish Pattern," (Appendix I) provides two live demonstrations of this technique with nail-biting and anger—one in the auditory system—as well as some discussion. Richard Bandler's client session videotape "Anticipatory Loss" (Appendix II) provides another demonstration.

In the size/brightness swish, the cue image begins big and bright, and then quickly becomes small and dim. At the same time the desired self-image begins small and dim and quickly becomes big and bright. By changing submodalities in this way, the person's attention is quickly drawn from the cue to the desired self-image by a process called chaining: linking two experiences together.

The three major elements of the swish are:
1. Selecting the cue to swish from.
2. Developing a desired self-image that is attractive and motivating.
3. Using powerful submodality shifts to link the two together.

Cue Selection

Since the cue is the trigger that will begin the swish, it's important to identify a cue that will work. If you use an inappropriate cue, the swish may work perfectly, but at irrelevant times and places.

Dependability.   Select a cue image that will *always be there* just before the problem behavior occurs. If you do a swish and find that the problem behavior is significantly reduced but not eliminated, you can explore the possibility that there is an additional cue that still triggers the problem behavior. For instance, one of our students did a swish on a smoker, who immediately cut down from a pack a day to about five cigarettes a day. He no longer carried his own cigarettes, but he would occasionally ask for a cigarette from friends. The cue image he had used was seeing his hand taking a cigarette "out of a pack," and the swish worked perfectly whenever that cue occurred. However, the sight of taking a cigarette "from someone else's hand" did not trigger the swish. His brain didn't automatically generalize from one situation to the other. Some people would automatically generalize in this way, but you can't count on it. When the cue image was redescribed as "seeing a cigarette in your hand" and he used the swish again, his smoking stopped completely.

Another example of the cue image being too specific is a client who completely stopped smoking with his right hand, but started with his left hand! When most people hear "see your hand with a cigarette," they will understand this to mean *either* hand. This client made a distinction between the two hands; the swish worked perfectly for the right hand, but not at all for the left.

A woman who picked her fingernail cuticles used an image of her *two* hands picking at each other as a cue. That behavior stopped, but she found that each hand still picked at the nails on the same hand! When she swished again using an image of her hands picking at themselves, that behavior also stopped.

Use of Internal Cue Image.   If many different external environmental cues all trigger an internal state, and this internal state in turn triggers the unwanted response, it is often much simpler and more economical to use a dependable *internal* image as the cue. In Richard Bandler's videotape "Anticipatory Loss" (see Appendix II), he used the client's internal picture of zooming in on an injured friend as the cue picture, rather than an external cue, such as looking at a clock and noticing that a friend was a half-hour late. Since this internal image was always present just before she panicked, it's a dependable cue for the swish.

This client said that sometimes her internal picture was somewhat different: "looking out at the world . . . and there's no one there." Although Richard did not explicitly swish with this second image, to her it was "the same'' as the first image, so she unconsciously generalized the swish to this image, too.

Cue Image Usually Associated.   If the cue image is of an external real-world cue, such as seeing your hand with a cigarette, it should *always be associated*, so that it is as similar as possible to what you will actually encounter in the real world. This ensures that the real world cue will trigger the swish mechanism that is based on the internal picture of that same cue.

If the cue is an internal image that dependably triggers the unwanted behavioral response, it should be *exactly as the person experiences it when it produces the unwanted response*. One client complained of feeling inadequate in a number of different situations. In each of these situations she was in effect doing a reverse swish on herself: she flashed an image of herself (dissociated) falling apart and acting incompetently. Since she saw this image of herself in each of the contexts she wanted to change, I had her use this dissociated internal image as the cue. She reported later that this made a major shift, allowing her to feel and act resourceful.

Desired Self-image.

The desired self-image is ''the you with more choices, for whom this unwanted behavior/response is not a problem.'' There are a number of elements that make this image a powerful motivator for change.

Self-image Always Dissociated   It's essential that the desired self-image *be dissociated*, in order to make it motivating. You are drawn *toward* this image when it is dissociated. If you are associated into it, you are already there, so it's not motivating. If you swished to an associated image, you would be throwing away one of the most powerful elements of the pattern. This point is discussed at some length in *Using Your Brain*. *Sometimes* swishing to an associated image will work to solve a problem, but it won't be nearly as powerful or as *generative*. The results will be more like the results of straight chaining, or mapping across from one situation to another. When you map across, you generally end up associated into some specific resource state.

In the process of developing the desired self-image, it is sometimes useful to *temporarily* associate into it to get the feel of what it would be like to be this person. This is especially true if the client says something like, ''I can see the me with more choices, but I have no idea what that would be like; I don't know if I'd like that or not." Associating into this image temporarily can provide information about how nice it would be. Then when you swish toward the dissociated image it will be more motivating.

Association is also useful if the person can't see himself with enough choices to overcome the problem. You can ask him to see himself with a *few* more creative resources, and then have him associate into this image. "Since you now have these additional creative resources, you can create an even more powerful and appropriate desired self-image." You can repeat this process as many times as you need to, in order to chunk down the task of developing the desired self-image.

Qualities vs Specific Behaviors.   The self-image is of *qualities*, not specific behaviors. You see yourself with *capabilities* and *choices*, rather than specific alternative behaviors to do.

This distinction is not obvious to some clients. One way to make it clear is to say, "Think of something that you do well, such as skiing. If you were looking at a snapshot of yourself, you would know by looking at it that this person knew how to ski, even though you are not actually skiing in the picture."

Another way to explain the difference is to say, "Let's imagine I tell you that I'm going to throw this pen to you in a few minutes, in a way that will make it easy for you to catch it. When you make a picture of yourself able to catch the pen, you don't know exactly how you will catch the pen— reaching up, down, or to the side, etc.—because that will depend on how I throw it. You know that you will be able to catch it, even though you don't know exactly how you'll do it." .

"If you imagine yourself ordering a meal in a restaurant a week from now, you don't know what you'll order, because that will depend upon how hungry you feel at the time and what's available on the menu. Nevertheless, you can see that you are confident of being able to order appropriately when you're actually in the restaurant."

Even these explanations didn't make it clear to one workshop participant, so I pointed to a well-dressed, very alert woman in the front row. "Look at that woman. Isn't it obvious from her dress, her posture, the way she moves and looks at you, that here is a woman with a wide range of abilities and choices?" If you don't have a handy participant to point to, you could ask the client to think of someone he admires, and then use the same approach.

This image of yourself with the *qualities* of choice and capability draws you toward generating a variety of behaviors that are appropriate to the problem situation. If you want to program a *specific* behavior, it is simpler to use some other NLP technique, such as the new behavior generator. This is also discussed in considerable detail in *Using Your Brain*.

Ecology.   There are several elements in the swish that tend to make it ecological. The fact that you use a desired self-image with *qualities* rather than with a specific solution means that the change is more likely to be ecological. Since any specific solution is much more likely to have ecological problems associated with it, "the you for whom this is no longer a problem" provides ecological protection. If the client asks for a specific solution, keep in mind that this is his conscious mind talking, and that the reason he doesn't already have this solution installed may be that it is somehow inappropriate, and some other part of him knows this. By programming in *qualities*, you provide much more flexibility in *how* to reach the desired outcome. You see someone who could generate many specific alternate behaviors in response to the needs of the situation.

Another way that ecology is built into the swish is that the desired self-image is created with considerable participation of the person's unconscious mind. Although the initial direction is conscious, the resulting image is autonomous and unconscious: you mobilize unconscious resources to generate an image that satisfies other unconscious outcomes. If you don't believe this, get such an image and then try to change it consciously. You may be able to change it temporarily, but it will usually change back as soon as your conscious attention goes elsewhere.

This image of yourself with qualities and abilities mobilizes all your unconscious resources to generate many specific behaviors, adapting to the situation. A swish often reorganizes a person's behavior in a matter of seconds, and most people who have been swished successfully report that they have no conscious information about what the reorganization was, or how they were able to accomplish it.

Although these factors all tend to make the swish ecological, they depend on the abilities of the client's unconscious mind. Sometimes it may need a little help and direction.

Accessing Appropriate Resources.   When you tell the client "See the you for whom this isn't a problem," some people will immediately be able to visualize a person with the kind of resources to handle the situation. Others will need some help to enable them to see the kind of person who has the resources that will make a difference. Often you can make some guesses about which resources would benefit the client. Sometimes your client can't think of any resources that would make a difference, but you can. When you suggest resources to the client, you can watch him, and amplify what the client responds to positively. When you suggest something the client doesn't respond to, drop it.

For example, if you are doing a swish with someone who loses her temper at "trivial" things, you could say "If it's appropriate, you can add in the ability to be compassionate toward other people, and expect ahead of time that they will sometimes make mistakes. Or, perhaps this you is better able to see things from the other person's point of view, and understand how that person acted the way she did. Maybe this you doesn't need to assign blame when something goes wrong, but instead just notices that someone else has a different perspective, and immediately starts to think about what might make the situation work for both of you." You can pack a lot of resources into one image. Your guideline in offering these suggestions is *not* "Are these the *right* resources?" but "Are these words helping the client see something that looks more and more resourceful and attractive?"

Another way to think about this is that you are adding specific resources into the desired self-image which satisfy the positive intent of the old response. Doing this insures that your work will be ecological. If someone smokes to relax and to take a short break from work, you can say, "See the you for whom smoking is irrelevant. This is the you who has *lots* of choices about how to relax and take a break. You may not know exactly *how* he does these things, but you can see by looking at him that this is a person with lots of choices about how to relax."

When a swish works partially, you can ask about the *contexts* where it did and didn't work. If someone says, "I was fine alone in my office, but in the department meeting all those people really got on my nerves," you can guess that he needs more choices about dealing with other people. A little questioning will provide even more specific information about what additional qualities or abilities need to be added into the desired self-image.

Make Sure the Image is Balanced.   Sometimes a person's desired self-image is initially too extreme. If it's *too* strong, for instance, you may need to adjust it by adding in some gentleness, humility, or compassion to make it fully acceptable to all parts of the person. One woman who wanted a better choice than losing her temper, saw the her who was "completely calm at all times." She seemed to be picturing someone who would do just fine in heaven, but wouldn't survive very well on earth. I suggested that she check to "make sure that this is someone who can keep her eye on her *outcomes*, and who has the flexibility to act angry at times when she thinks that will best serve her outcomes, or to be able to stand up for what she wants at times, in addition to being calm. This could be someone who has ways of dealing with things that used to be irritating that you, sitting here, don't have any inkling of. But for her it's easy."

Another woman saw a "her" that seemed *too* perfect. I suggested that she add in the quality of being able to laugh at her own mistakes and learn from them.

Checking for Ecology.   Putting appropriate resources in the desired self representation preserves ecology. If you want to, you can explicitly check for ecology as you develop the desired self-image. "As you look at that you who has more abilities, and no longer has that problem, do you mind if you end up being that person?" It's useful to check all major life contexts, and all major representational systems. "How will this new you behave with family? . . . At work? . . . At play? . . . As you observe this person, is there anything that you see, hear, or feel that alerts you to any possible problems?" Whenever you encounter objections, you can make appropriate adjustments in the self-image until it's satisfactory.

Reality Constraints.   Like a compelling future image, the self-image has to satisfy the person's criteria about what he responds to as real or possible. Even if you like the image, you won't respond to it much if you think of it as unreal or unlikely. In that case you need to know which submodalities make it unreal, and make adjustments until it's at least a believable possibility.

About a year ago, I (Connirae) did the swish with Kate, who had witnessed a multiple fatality accident. Kate barely missed being a victim herself. After that she panicked every time she had to drive, and was preoccupied with the accident at other times. Zooming in on the face of one of the accident victims was what made her panic, so I designed a swish for her starting with this cue. It was easy to get Kate to make an image of "the her for whom this wasn't a difficulty," but Kate didn't look attracted to the image. Kate said the image "didn't seem real." It turned out that she was making an image of the her who had taken CPR training, and was medically knowledgeable. While this Kate would know what to do, she seemed unreal, since Kate didn't actually know CPR. Kate had assumed that this was necessary for her to feel resourceful.

It seemed to me unneccessary and unuseful for someone to feel panicked and out of control just because she doesn't have an M.D. Many people have no medical knowledge, and yet don't get panicked by accidents, so I know that panic is not a neccessary response. Kate seemed to be thinking of this as an either/or situation: either she had to be completely medically competent so that she could feel in control, or she had to feel totally out of control.

Kate's objection told me exactly what to do next. I suggested that rather than seeing the Kate who could do CPR, she could see "the you who may not know any more about medicine than you do sitting here now, but she has the resources to deal with a difficult situation as best she can, given what she knows. Perhaps this is the Kate who can walk into an emergency and decide on the spot how she can be most useful. Panic is irrelevant to her, because she knows how to quickly and calmly assess what she can do, and not try to do anything she knows she can't do. What this Kate knows is not medicine, it's how to use whatever information and skills she has to act in the best way possible. She may make mistakes once in a while—as all people do—but she also has the resources to learn from them, and use the learning next time." As I talked, Kate's face began to look more and more pleased with, and attracted to, the Kate of the future that she was seeing in her mind's eye.

After doing the swish, Kate was pleased that she could drive comfortably, no longer preoccupied with accidents. During the next few months, she encountered two accidents that she was able to respond to resourcefully and calmly.

Contextualization. In most cases you want the desired change to generalize fully to all areas of the person's life. This is accomplished by using a self-image that is *un*contextualized: the image of yourself should have as little context as possible. No surroundings at all is ideal. However, since some people don't like to see themselves floating in space, it can be helpful to have a very vague generalized background or a surface to stand on.

If you do create an image of yourself in a specific context, change may be restricted to that context and not generalize to others. One man created a self-image of himself in the seminar room. After he was swished he had no desire to smoke in the seminar room, no matter how long he was there. However, the moment he left that room, the desire came back. Some people will generalize widely even if they see themselves in a specific context, but others will not. Inappropriate contextualization is another common reason for getting incomplete results with the swish.

You could use the same principle to restrict a change to only one, or a few, specific contexts. However, it's much more generative, and ecologically safer, to add the ability to discriminate into the self-image. "This is the you who has the ability to notice when and where it will be useful to utilize these new choices, and when and where it may be more useful to continue to use old behaviors."

Linking The Two Images

Once you have selected the cue image, and developed a motivating desired self-image, your task is to link them together using any two submodalities that are impactful to the person. The following conditions help make this linkage as powerful as possible.

Simultaneity.   It would be possible to have the cue image first become small and dim, and *then* have the self-image grow large and bright. If you do this, the swish may still work, but the chaining effect is weakened by sequencing the two changes. It is much better to have the two changes occur at the same time, so that *as* your response to the cue decreases, your response to the self-image increases *simultaneously*. If you use sequential changes, make sure that something about the way you do it makes a secure link between the two. For instance, you could put the self-image picture on the back side of the cue picture, and then have the cue picture tilt down, turn over, and tilt up again to reveal the self-image. Although the changes are sequential, the first is tied to the second by being part of the same object that turns over in space. If the cue picture tilted down in one location and the self-image picture tilted up in another location, the linkage would be much weaker.

Direction.   It is absolutely essential to *swish in one direction only*: from the cue to the desired self-image. This is accomplished by an interruption at the end of each swish, such as blanking your internal visual screen, or opening your eyes. There are already too many people who swish themselves in the opposite direction: they imagine themselves capable of doing something and then immediately think of some personal failure or misfortune (past or imagined future) and get discouraged. If you run the swish backward, you can make someone *less* capable rather than more. And if you swish someone in both directions they can end up going in circles!

Speed.   Make sure the actual exchange of images occurs as quickly as possible. You can take as long as you want setting up the initial conditions, and after the swish you can take time to enjoy the self-image, but the transition between the two should take only a second or less.

Sometimes it's easiest to start the client doing the swish slowly, making sure that he knows exactly what to do. Then you can speed him up by saying, "That's fine, now do it faster," "Even faster," etc., until you can see that he is doing it very quickly. If he objects that he can't consciously do it faster, you can say, "That's fine; your brain already knows what to do now. You can just start at the beginning, and your unconscious mind can do the swish part more completely and thoroughly than you would be able to consciously. We want it to become unconscious as quickly as possible anyway." Of course you need to observe the client carefully to verify that his nonverbal behavior indicates that he is actually doing what you asked. You can even tell someone to *pretend* to do the swish faster, as long as you use nonverbal feedback to verify that he is going through the process behaviorally.

Repetition.   Five repetitions are usually sufficient to install a swish. Sometimes it only takes one or two times. If you do it ten times rapidly and it doesn't work, more repetition isn't likely to help; you probably need to make some other adjustments to make it work.

Calibration to Submodality Accessing Cues.   The best way to be sure that someone is actually doing the swish is by calibrating to the characteristic subtle nonverbal behaviors that accompany the different submodality shifts. For instance, when an image moves rapidly closer, your head tends to move straight back, your eyes widen a bit, and your overall muscle tone increases. When an image moves away, your head tends to move forward, the eyes narrow slightly, and your muscles relax a little.

Although it's tedious to verbally describe these nonverbal accessing cues, you can easily discover them for yourself by using the following procedure. Get a willing friend, sit facing him to one side, and ask him to think of an image that is emotionally neutral. If you use an emotionally charged picture, the many nonverbal shifts resulting from the feeling changes will make it difficult to distinguish the changes that are associated with the submodality shifts alone. When your friend has chosen a neutral image, ask him to shift *one* specific submodality in both directions: "Make that image bigger, . . . Now make it smaller. . . ." and observe the nonverbal shifts. Shifting quickly from one extreme to the other will increase the contrast, making the nonverbal shifts easier to observe. Changes in head position are usually the easiest to observe; there are also changes in pupil size and in the muscles around the eyes, breathing shifts, overall muscle tone changes, etc. People differ in their expressiveness; these cues will be very obvious in some people and much subtler in others. A more expressive person will make your initial learning much easier.

It's important to verify that your subject changes *only* the submodality you asked him to change. If his picture automatically becomes more colorful when it gets bigger, you will see cues resulting from *both* these submodality shifts, and this will be confusing to you.

If you have fine awareness of your own kinesthetic movements, you can do the same kind of experimenting with yourself. Adjust one submodality of a neutral picture in both directions, and *feel* how your own muscles shift as you do this.

Being able to observe and identify submodality accessing cues makes your work elegant. You can use them to gather information when your client isn't aware of submodalities and can't report them. Since they provide you with detailed ongoing feedback about your client's internal processes, you can also use them to verify that the client is doing what you asked him to do.

Nonverbal Direction. Using your own behavior to demonstrate the process is the best way to make it easy for the client to do the swish. You can use your hand to indicate the size and location of the images for the set-up, and move your hand to indicate the speed and direction of change.

We usually prefer to let the client learn how to do her own swish. Once she knows how to do it, we only make sure that she does it fast enough. However, you can also use nonverbal directions to run the swish for the client. If you make a "swish" sound as you move your hands to demonstrate, that also becomes an anchor for the speed of the transition. Once that is set up, you can often run the repetitions of the swish simply by repeating those movements and sounds, and you can observe the person responding unconsciously. This is particularly useful for clients who aren't adept at steering their own brains, or for covert work.

When you do this, *be sure that your gestures are appropriate from the client's point of view.* Let's say you are facing the client and say, "Move that picture away." If you move you hand away from your own face, it will move *closer* to your client's face, and this is incongruent with your verbal instruction. Be sure to make gestures that are appropriate for the client, even though it may not be appropriate to your own position. An easy way to avoid this problem is to sit alongside the client and face in the same direction. Then your gestures can be appropriate for both of you.

If you internally do the same process that you are asking your client to do, your own accessing cues will also unconsciously communicate to the client what to do. We can't overemphasize the importance of your nonverbal behavior. Incongruence can spoil an intervention, and congruence can make your work very easy.

Reference Experiences.   Another way to make a swish easy is to access a reference experience from the real world that is analagous to the effect you want to create. This can range from simple figures of speech like, "Let the color *wash* out of that picture," to more complex metaphorical accesses:

"Have you ever seen a drop of light oil or gasoline land on a water surface, and watched that droplet quickly spread and cover it with vibrant color? That's what I want you to do. That small dot will quickly spread like a drop of oil into a colorful image of yourself as you want to be."

"Imagine that the cue picture is a thin watercolor painting that is painted over an oil painting of yourself as you want to be. A downpour comes and quickly washes away the watercolor, revealing the oil painting underneath."

When doing a distance swish, some people have trouble synchronizing the simultaneous movements of the two images. You can say, "Pretend there is a string that goes from that cue picture around a pulley behind your head, and back out to the other picture. As the first picture moves away, that string will automatically pull the second picture toward you at the same speed."

"Imagine that you are in a dark room, and that there is a bright light over your head, but no lights farther away. As that first picture moves away from you and the light, it will automatically become dimmer. As that second picture moves toward you and the light, it will automatically get brighter."

Doing it the Client's Way.   The more the swish is congruent with what the client can already easily do in his mind, the easier it will be for him to do it, and the more effective it will be.

If you can't think of an appropriate reference experience, often your client can provide it. "What's an easy way for you to make that colorful picture colorless?" "Oh, I know, I can pretend the color is on a transparency, so I can just peel it off." "Well, if the color was a liquid it would just drain out if I pulled the plug, like water out of sand." By using the client's resources in this way you make sure that the swish will be easy for him to do, and you also enrich your own repertoire of transition methods.

When Richard Bandler first taught the standard size/brightness swish, he told people to place the small dark self-image picture in the lower left-hand corner of the big bright cue picture. A year later he said to put it in the lower right-hand corner. We have found that many people find it easier to put it somewhere in the center. You can even say, "Pick some small dark area, like a button, or a shadowed area, and let the self-image picture blossom quickly out of that, like a blooming flower." This utilizes a small dark area that already exists in the cue picture, eliminating the effort of adding the small dark picture to it. The more you can utilize your client's preferences and existing abilities, the easier it will be for both of you.

Testing. Although the ultimate and most dependable test is in the real world, you always want to test as thoroughly as possible *before* your client encounters the real world again. The best test of all is to behaviorally create a situation that is an example of the problem. In order to do this well, you need to test beforehand, to confirm that you know enough details to behaviorally produce the problem response in your client. If the client can't deal with scorn, sneeringly comment on his clothes before the swish, and afterwards comment about how sloppily he did it. If a woman can't stand being ignored, arrange for someone to come in and engage you in a conversation while you ignore her.

Although it's not quite as good as a behavioral test, you can always test by asking the client to think of the cue, and find out if it still produces the problem response. This kind of test is discussed in detail in *Using Your Brain*.

It's also possible to use "testing" to install or solidify the change you have just made, by using verbal and nonverbal presuppositions. Since one of the presuppositions of "trying" is that you will fail, when Richard Bandler says to his client in the "Anticipatory Loss" videotape, *"Try* to get the panic back," with an "offhand" tone of voice, he is strongly implying that she won't be able to. When he says, "Try it one more time, *to be sure,*" he is future-pacing confidence that she won't be able to panic in the future. If you are testing as a scientist, you want to do it in a very neutral way: "Make that picture again. . . . What happens?" However, if you want to help someone solidify a change, you may as well use any verbal or nonverbal patterns you know which will support that change.

Designer Swishes

The size/brightness swish arbitrarily uses size and brightness to run the swish. Although this is effective about 70% of the time, some people don't respond much to size or brightness. A few people respond more intensely to a dim image than a bright one. If so, using brightness in the usual way will weaken the swish, not strengthen it.

Even though someone may respond to size and brightness in many contexts, her problem may be caused by an *auditory* cue. A voice, or some other sound, may produce the undesired response. You could always overlap to a visual cue, "Listen to that voice; if that voice were a picture, what would it look like?" and then do a swish in the visual system. However, when the cue is auditory, it's much more elegant and powerful to create a swish in the auditory system itself.

Auditory Swish Example.   To swish auditorily, you first ask questions to find out which auditory submodalities (either internal or external) make the cue powerful. "What is it that makes it impossible for you to ignore that sound?" "Well, sometimes it's not very loud and I can ignore it, but when it's loud, it drives me up the wall. When it gets louder, it gets closer too, and that really bugs me."

The next step is to test to find out if volume and distance can be used to change the person's response. "Listen to it, and make it louder. . . . Now make it softer. . . . Does that change your response?" As usual, you are much more interested in observing his nonverbal response than in hearing his conscious verbal response. "Next try changing the distance of that sound. Keep the volume the same, but move it in closer. . . . Now move it farther away. . . . Does that change your response?

Since nearly everyone responds strongly to auditory volume and proximity, let's assume your testing confirms that these submodalities are powerful for the person. You now know the auditory cue, and how to use two auditory submodalities to increase or decrease your client's response to it.

The next step is to help the client develop the representation of herself with more choices in the *auditory* system. As before, this self-voice will be dissociated, so that she is drawn to it. "Hear what your voice would sound like if you had so many additional choices and abilities that this situation is no longer be a problem for you. Hear that voice out there, at some distance from you, as if it were someone else speaking to you. What are the qualities of this voice as you hear it?" Develop this voice until the client is powerfully attracted to it.

Next you need to test the same submodalities that you found in the auditory cue, to find out how tonality and volume affect the intensity of the client's response to the self-voice. "Make this voice louder. . . . Does that make your response more intense?" "Now make this voice softer. . . . Does that make your response less intense?" Usually a person will respond most intensely to a resourceful self-voice at a *moderate* volume. If the resourceful voice gets too loud, most people switch to an *unpleasant* response, instead of further intensifying the pleasant response.

Overall, an effective swish pattern will *decrease the response to the cue*, and simultaneously *increase the response to the desired self-representation*. If possible, find two powerful submodalities that work the same way for the cue sound and the desired self-voice. In this example, let's assume that closeness and increase in volume *increase* the client's response to both the cue and the desired self-voice.

In this case the cue will start at maximum intensity: loud volume and close. The volume will quickly fade away as the cue gets more distant, decreasing the client's response.

The desired self-voice will simultaneously start out at minimum intensity, very softly at a distance, and then move in closer and louder *to the volume and distance at which the client has the most powerfully positive response*. As with any other swish, you would end with silence, or listening externally, and then repeat the swish process until it has been done five times rapidly, before testing.

Sometimes the person's response to the volume of this resourceful self-voice is the *opposite* of her response to the cue. A louder volume sometimes makes the person respond *less*. While a softer volume makes the person respond *more*. In the size/brightness swish we assume that increasing brightness will increase the intensity of response to *both* the cue image and the desired self-image. When there is an *inverse* relationship with other submodalities, the swish you design has to be adjusted accordingly.

Now let's assume that while loud volume increases the response to the cue, it *decreases* the response to the self-voice; the self-voice is most compelling at *low* volume. Then you would need to swish differently. Both the cue and the desired self-voice would start out at high volume and then become soft. As before, the cue will move off to the distance, as the self-voice moves in close. The cue will fade away completely, and you will be left with the self-voice at the volume and tonality to which you respond most intensely.

Designer Swish Outline

1. Identify the problem or limitation: "What do you want to change? How are you broken? What are you dissatisfied with?"

2. Gather information: Use Richard Bandler's "accomplishment" frame: "Let's say I had to fill in for you for a day. To do a complete job, I would have to do your limitation. Teach me how to do it." You need to find out *when* to do it (the cue), and *how* to do it (the process). In particular, you need to know *which two analogue submodalities change the cue, and how they change in order to create the problem*. Essentially you are finding out how the client *already* swishes himself, so you can use the same kind of process to swish him somewhere else.

3. Test the cue: When you think you know how to do this, test by trying it out yourself. If you do what your client does, is your response similar? Your client may be doing something *else* that you don't know about yet, or he may be organized differently from you, so it will not work for you in the same way *unless* you take on his submodality change relationships.

When you get the same response as your client, that doesn't necessarily mean your information is correct, but it's a good indication. When you try doing what your client does, it often makes perfect sense that he responds the way he does. If it doesn't make sense, gather more information to find out what you may be missing.

4. Develop the desired self-representation and test: First develop the desired self-representation in the same system as the cue, and then find out how the same two analogue submodalities affect it. "How does your response to seeing yourself with more choices change when you increase and decrease that specific submodality?"

5. Review data: At this point you should have the following:

a. The cue representation which is dependably present, and which triggers the limitation, and how two powerful analogue submodalties can be used to vary the intensity of the problem response.

b. The desired self-representation in the same representational system as the cue, and how the same two submodalities can be used to increase or decrease the client's response to the desired self-image representation.

6. Plan: how to use these two submodalities to link the cue to the self-representation. It's easiest and safest to plan *separately* for the cue and for the self-representation.

a. Cue.   Determine how you can shift these two submodalities to begin with an intense response to the cue and then decrease this response.

b. Self-representation.   Determine how you can shift these same two submodalities to begin with a low-intensity response and then increase the response to maximum intensity.

c. Put a and b together to determine the beginning state for both cue and self-representation, and the transitions that will take you to the ending state for both.

Kinesthetic Swish.   Although it's easier for most people to do a visual or auditory swish, you can also swish in the kinesthetic system as long as you are very careful to use *tactile* kinesthetics and not meta-kinesthetics. The cue could be the feeling of someone's hand on your body, or the feel of breath on your neck, for instance, but *not* the meta-kinesthetic feeling response of disgust or fear. You can discover which tactile submodalities—pressure, extent, location, texture, movement, duration, temperature, frequency, etc.—can be used to increase/decrease the problem response for a swish.

The self-representation is dissociated, as if you are reaching out and touching your own body in space in front of you, feeling the easy relaxed strength in this capable you, with the straight spine and balance, or however you represent kinesthetic capability. Then you can use submodalities to swish from the tactile sensations of the cue to the tactile sensations of the self-representation, just as you would in the visual or auditory system.

Sometimes when swishing in the kinesthetic system, it's useful to swish *both* to an associated and to a dissociated desired self-feeling, sequentially. This is different from what we do in a visual or auditory swish, in which we always end with a *dissociated* self-representation. When I have done a kinesthetic swish ending with a dissociated self, sometimes the person complained that they didn't have a new feeling to replace the old one *in the same location*. When I added a swish to the *associated* kinesthetic feelings, they were satisfied. Since the feelings of the *associated* new self extend over your entire body, they will replace the original cue feelings, whatever their location.

Mixed-system Swish

You could also swish in two systems at once, for instance using one visual submodality and one auditory submodality. We recommend against this, unless you have compelling evidence that the two most powerful submodalities are in two different representational systems, *and* your client can do the task easily. It's usually easier for the client if you pick the one representational system that seems most powerful for the client, and swish in that representational system. Then you can test to find out if that swish automatically changed the submodality in the other representational system also. If not, you can also do a swish in the other representational system.

The swish is an incredibly powerful pattern which can be used for a wide variety of problems. Although it appears simple, it is actually quite complex. Careful attention to all the details we have discussed will make it possible for you to create powerful swishes that will change your clients profoundly with little effort.

However, keep in mind that all these words only point to the reality of you working with a client. Your client's experience is the ultimate authority. Overall, your goal is to find the cue that triggers the problem behavior/response and use that to send his brain in a more useful direction. Do anything you can to accomplish that.

Examples

1. Bobbi, the second demonstration client in our videotape "The Swish Pattern" (see Appendix I) was very sensitive to her daughter's voice in certain situations. Connirae found that volume and panoramic vs. point source of the sound were the most powerful submodalities. In the swish, her daughter's voice began loud and panoramic, and her desired self-voice started softly and as a point source. Then her daughter's voice faded away to a point source as her self-voice became panoramic and increased to optimum volume.

2. Amy strongly responded to her ex-husband's voice. The moment she thought of it, the tears would start—which initially made it a little difficult to gather information! Steve found that volume was one submodality that powerfully affected her response; lowering the volume of the voice made it much easier to gather more information.

The other, and more powerful, submodality turned out to be location in space. As Amy described it, "The left side is for people; the right side is for things," a very uncommon arrangement. If she moved her ex-husband's voice from near her left ear to near her right ear, her response to it decreased dramatically. Her response to her capable self-voice changed in the same way. Steve swished her by starting with her ex-husband's voice loud and near her left ear, and her self-voice at very low volume near her right ear. As the voices quickly exchanged locations, her ex-husband's voice faded away and her self-voice rose to optimum volume. The first time Amy did this, her face broke into an enormous grin. These submodalities were so powerful for her that a single swish changed her permanently.

3. George had two pictures of "what is" and "what was" which alternated as if they were rotating on a rolodex file. Speed and size increased his response of feeling depressed. George's group was stumped at how to create a swish, since the speed of the two images alternating, was the most powerful submodality for George in creating depression, and the desired self-image is usually only one picture. Connirae had George create *two* alternating desired self-images, in order to match the cue: one of himself able to get what he wanted, and the other of himself able to get even *more* of what he wanted. When George alternated these two images, he got a powerfully positive response. The swish started with the two cue pictures large, and alternating very fast. This slowed and shrank down as a self-image rolodex which had started small and still, got larger and moved faster.

4. When Daniel's wife would make a critical comment, he would think of saying something back to her, and see his words "bouncing off her and toward me like a laser light that wipes me out." Speed and size were the major submodalities. When we swished him, this cue picture shrank and slowed down to a still picture, as the self-representation started as a small still picture which grew larger as it became a movie.

5. Ron complained that certain people made him angry. When he made the picture of the other person closer, we saw an increase in the response he didn't like, so we knew distance would be impactful. As we gathered information about what he needed to do to create this response, it became clear that his angry response could lead to violence. His body started leaning forward in "attack" mode, and we knew he had a history of physical violence.

Then we asked him to try making the cue image three-dimensional. Ron had a very strong response to doing this, but it was a *change in quality*, rather than just an increase or decrease in intensity. When Ron made the *cue* image three-dimensional, his whole body softened and relaxed. He looked more responsive to the other person, without even making a self-image who could handle this kind of situation. Ron reported that 3-D made the other person look much more like a whole complete person, rather than a flat image that was easier to get mad at.

When doing the swish, we usually use submodalities that shift intensity only. We thought 3-D was well-worth using with Ron, since this submodality itself seemed to be a very useful resource.

As we prepared to do a swish with Ron, he objected. "If we do this, I can't keep everyone out there." We suggested that he add qualities into the image of "the new Ron" giving him resources to get along with people up close, as well as the ability to keep people distant when he wants to. "See the Ron who can decide when he wants closeness, and when he wants distance, and all the possibilities in between. This Ron can have the ability to see others as whole people, to recognize their positive and negative qualities at the same time, so that he can understand them more completely and respond more effectively."

This helped, but Ron still objected:

"I want a way to be safe, you're taking away my way to be safe. I want another way to be safe."

When we questioned Ron "safe from what? How do you want to be safe?" he couldn't answer us. So we said the following:

"You have a sense of what safety means to you, even though you can't put it into words (using Ron's gesture for safety). . . . Now close your eyes and let yourself unconsciously get a sense of what that safety is for you. . . . And let that unconscious knowledge transfer itself into the image of that Ron, who can be safe in *other* ways. You don't even need to know exactly how he's going to be safe; you don't need to know exactly which additional choices he has. But you can recognize, when you look at him, that he has the ability to have that kind of safety, . . . and not be satisfied until you can see in that picture that he is safe—as safe as any human can be. . . . And my guess is that he'll be far safer than the old Ron, because he'll be safe in a more solid, more real, more 3-dimensional sort of way. . . ."

When we asked, "How does that look up there? When you look at him do you know that he's safe?" Ron said, "Yes, that looks nice and safe, and a lot of other things, too."

We then assisted Ron in swishing from a close flat cue image of the other person's face that went off into the distance as it became 3-D, to a desired self-image which began far away and flat, and moved in close as it became 3-D. Ron reported later that he had much more space in his life overall, and less often felt trapped or "boxed-in."

Ron's internal experience fits with our knowledge of what makes it possible for violence to occur on a large scale, as well as in families. When a country gears up for war, cartoonists depict the enemy as less than human. They become flat cartoon characters, or monsters. When we look at other people as three-dimensional fully human beings like ourselves, it's much more difficult to be violent.

6. Mary came to see me (Connirae) for weight loss. She said she had tried lots of things, and wasn't able to lose weight. She was convinced that the problem was glandular, since nothing else had worked, but wanted to try NLP.

When I asked her if she overate, she said she didn't think so. I asked her if there were any particular foods that she ate in a compulsive sort of way. She said she didn't think so, but maybe she overate doughnuts. I wasn't getting very much verbal or nonverbal response, but went ahead gathering information, and did a compulsion blowout followed by a swish.

The next week I spoke to Mary on the phone. She said, "After that session, I was a completely different person for four days. I lost eight pounds without trying, and felt completely different, and then the whole thing fell apart." I asked her if she had any idea what had made everything fall apart. She said she didn't, so we set up another appointment to explore what needed to be done next.

At this next session, I asked again, "What do you think happened to make your new choices fall apart?"

"I don't know."

"Well, guess."

"I'd have to completely make it up. It doesn't seem like anything was different in my life to make it fall apart."

"Great, go ahead and make it up."

"I suppose it could be the usual thing with my son, or that I've been thinking lately that I'm not sure I'm doing anything worthwhile in my life. Then, too, my family living situation is up in the air now, because we're not sure if we're going to be moving to Australia. I suppose it could be something to do with that." She also mentioned one additional stressor that I don't remember. This sounded like enough content for years of traditional therapy.

I started by asking her what she meant by "the usual thing with my son.'' Her response was a long story about how she had a son from a previous marriage who was diagnosed manic-depressive, and had been in and out of mental hospitals for years. She felt very responsible for this son's existence—it was her fault that she had brought a manic-depressive son into the world. She was convinced that manic depression is genetic, and her ex-husband was manic-depressive, so she thought she should have known better than to have a child with him. This son had been calling her up on the phone and threatening suicide. She said, in effect, ''It's my fault that this problem exists, and nothing can be done about it.''

As she described her problems, her nonverbal response was strongest when talking about her son, so I decided to work on that. When he called on the phone, she would imagine his face as he talked to her. As soon as she imagined his face, she collapsed into an unresourceful state, so I decided to use this cue to help her construct a swish. I asked her to ''Let an image emerge of the you who can deal resourcefully with *this* situation— the Mary for whom this is not a problem.''

Mary said, ''OK, I see her,'' but she didn't look very enthusiastic about what she saw. It was clear to me from her nonverbal response that the image she was seeing would not be resourceful enough to handle the situation she had described to me. I began to mention additional resources that she might want to add:

''I'd like you to take time to think about what additional resources you might want that Mary to have, so that you end up seeing someone even more attractive to you. I'm not sure what resources she would find particularly valuable, but you might consider whether she could use the ability to forgive herself for past mistakes—the ability to put the past behind her—to notice what she doesn't like about her past behavior, and to learn from it. She doesn't have to wallow around in the past. She can go on, and use her past mistakes as resources for being more and more of the person she wants to be.'' This got a positive response from Mary, so I had her add in this resource.

''And perhaps this Mary is someone with more choices about dealing with her son. You can have that sense about her, without knowing specifically what those choices are. Maybe this Mary is someone who can let her son rely more on his own resources, and not respond with guilt when he threatens her with suicide. She doesn't have to feel guilty, because that would only make things worse for him.

''And I know you have a young daughter now, and a marriage you're happy with. Perhaps this resourceful you is someone who knows how to be a model to your own daughter of what to do when you make mistakes.

Your daughter will make mistakes too, and she's looking to you to see how to deal with them. Do you want her to feel bad forever about a mistake she made in her past? Perhaps this Mary can demonstrate to her daughter a better way to deal with mistakes—to forgive herself, but not to forget—to learn from them.'' This got an even better response. Now Mary was glowing when she looked at the image of herself with choices, so I went ahead with the swish.

A few months later, I heard from Mary that this time the change had held up. She had lost weight without trying, and was very pleased with her new life.

IV

Shifting the Importance of Criteria

For some people, personal enjoyment or fun is so important that they never get around to accomplishing much. For others, success is so important that they never find time to relax and enjoy life. Words like "fun" and "success" indicate criteria— standards for evaluation that can be applied in a wide variety of situations. *Many* different activities can provide you with "fun," and many others can provide you with "success." Some activities can even provide you with both. Criteria are what you do something *for*. They are nominalizations such as "learning," "usefulness," "beauty," etc., that can be applied across contexts to evaluate outcomes. Criteria provide a useful way for us to organize our lives by generalizing.

Sometimes a criterion is too important or not important enough. Often criteria such as "being right," "pleasing others," or "power," take on such an importance in a person's life that he becomes unbalanced, and experiences personal difficulties or repeated complaints from others.

The Criteria Shift is a powerful pattern that allows you to change how important a criterion is. When you work with beliefs, quite often you change a limiting belief to its opposite. A person says, "I believe I can't learn," and you switch that to "I believe I *can* learn,"—a digital shift. However, when you're dealing with a person's criteria, you very seldom want to change them totally to their opposites. A complete reversal usually isn't necessary or desirable. Instead, you adjust the *relative* importance of criteria, making them more or less important. You make "being right" less important, or "having fun" more important—an analogue shift. This allows you to fine-tune the basis of your behavior, because we all behave in ways that fulfill the criteria that we hold important.

61

Yesterday someone said that people work to match their criteria or they don't work at all. That's a strong statement, but it's true. If an activity doesn't satisfy any of your criteria, it won't be interesting to you. Think of all the things that other people do eagerly that you find trivial or ridiculous. Somehow these activities must satisfy some criterion for them, but not for you.

Problems often arise in situations where two criteria are in conflict. You are faced with a choice of pleasing others or doing what you think is best, for example. That's where the ability to adjust criteria can make an important difference.

Before you can adjust criteria, you need to have some idea of how the brain *knows* what is important. How does a person's brain code criteria, so that when he thinks of "learning" or "fun," he automatically knows how important that is, and his behavior falls into line without having to consciously think about it? To find that out, the first step is to elicit a *hierarchy of criteria*: several criteria listed in order of importance. The second step will be to examine the submodality differences between these criteria, and the third step is to use those codings to adjust a problematic criterion. Because elicitation of criteria may be new for some of you, we're going to demonstrate. Even if you have done this before, I invite you to pay close attention; some people do it differently than the way we want you to do it.

Eliciting a Hierarchy of Criteria

Who would like his hierarchy of criteria elicited? . . .

Chris: I would.

Thanks, Chris. I want you to think of something trivial that you could do, but you wouldn't. For example, "I could stand on that chair, but I wouldn't," or "I could throw a piece of chalk across the room, but I wouldn't." Can you think of something relatively trivial like that?

Chris: Pick up a hitchhiker.

Fine. You could pick up a hitchhiker, but you wouldn't. Now, what stops you from picking up a hitchhiker?

Chris: A foreman who worked for me picked up a hitchhiker once who held him at gunpoint and made him drive two hundred miles, and I don't want the same thing to happen to me.

So the criterion involved here might be called "safety" or "survival." This is a much higher criterion than I wanted to start with. Since we're already dealing with life and death, we're probably near the top of Chris' hierarchy. For the sake of the demonstration, let's switch content. Think of something a *lot* more trivial, like you could stand on a chair, but you wouldn't, or you could pick your nose in public, but you wouldn't.

Chris: I could drink coffee, but I wouldn't.

Now, is that also going to jump you right to the top of your hierarchy? For some people, drinking coffee is the same as drinking arsenic; it violates a criterion involving health that is right up at the top of their hierarchy, so they don't do it. Is drinking coffee low enough for you?

Chris: Well, I can think of something lower than that: I could do the dishes today, but I wouldn't.

Great, that sounds low enough. "Doing the dishes" is a specific behavior. The next step is to identify the valued criterion that keeps him from doing the behavior. So Chris, what stops you from doing the dishes?

Chris: There aren't enough dishes to do.

OK, we still don't have a criterion, so I'll ask the question differently. Chris, what are you accomplishing by not doing the dishes?

Chris: Well, they'll accumulate until there's a reasonable amount to do, and then I'll do them all together.

And what will doing them all together at once accomplish?

Chris: It saves me time.

OK, so "saving time" is the relevant criterion. Notice that he's stated the criterion in the positive, that is, what he would be preserving or accomplishing, not what he would be avoiding. The same criterion could have been stated as "not wasting time." It's important to get all the criteria stated in the positive, without any negation. We'll discuss the reasons for this later.

Now we go to the next step. I want to find out what is more important to Chris than saving time. Chris, what would get you to do the dishes today anyway, even though you would be "wasting time" if you did?

Chris: If someone I didn't know was coming to visit.

Again, he's giving us a situation, an event, a circumstance: "somebody unknown coming to visit." For Chris, this is the additional *context* which determines that he will do the dishes. Now, what would you accomplish by doing the dishes in this situation? What's important to you here?

Chris: My visitor's perception of me would start off on a neutral basis.

Would it be accurate to say something like "I would create a certain impression?" (Chris frowns.) How might you rephrase that so it's accurate for you? You can see he's not happy with how I put it. It doesn't fit for him.

Chris: No, I don't particularly want to create any impression, positive or negative. Anyone who comes to my apartment has to take it the way it is. However, sloppy dishes are below my criterion of neutrality, of being neither too tidy nor too untidy.

All right, let's call this criterion "start with neutral impression." (Mm-hmm.) It's a bit long; I like to use one or two words if possible, but I think this conveys his meaning. He didn't like the way I phrased it, and I definitely want to use something that's meaningful to him. His first criterion is "saving time," the second "starting with a neutral impression." (See chart below.)

Behavior	Context	Criterion
1. not do dishes	not enough accumulated.	saving time
2. do dishes	someone new coming to visit.	start with neutral impression.
3. not do dishes		

Now, we want to identify an even higher criterion. Holding the context constant, we're going to negate the behavior again. Note that the context is *cumulative*: there are still only a few dirty dishes *and* somone unknown is coming to visit. You can *add* to the context each time, but you're not allowed to change what has already been specified. Chris, given this context, what would get you to *not* do the dishes, even though by not doing them you might not start on a neutral basis?

Chris: Oh, if I'd been cooking a meal.

And in that circumstance, what would you accomplish by leaving the dishes?

Chris: Well, if someone is coming over and the meal is on, I don't attempt to do all the dishes and have everything sparkling clean, because I like to serve everything hot.

Fine. And what's important about serving everything hot? We're still haven't got the criterion.

Chris: It's excellence of cooking—I'm a good cook.

Now we have a criterion. And I suspect that for you "excellence" in general is more important than "starting on a neutral basis" with people, which in turn is more important than "saving time."

Now, remember that there are still only a few dirty dishes, and someone unknown is coming to visit, *and* you're cooking a meal. In this context, what would get you to do the dishes anyway, even though that would violate your criterion of "excellence of cooking"?

Chris: If there was something unhygienic about leaving them.

"*Un*hygeinic" is a negation, so I want to switch that to something positive, like "preserving hygeine," as long as that restatement is acceptable to Chris. (Yes.) All right. Now, what would get you to leave the dishes undone, even though that would violate hygiene?

Chris: (long pause) If there was some crisis in the immediate vicinity, like a fire in my apartment building.

Now we're getting up to a highly-valued criterion. OK, what would you be preserving or accomplishing by responding to this crisis?

Chris: Preserving life.

We're up to "preserving life." Usually this is fairly high on a person's list.

Chris: "Preserving life" is actually a bit too high. It's more like "preserving safety," the safety of other people.

OK. You're "preserving safety" by responding to the crisis instead of doing the dishes. The stakes are certainly getting high on doing the dishes or not! Now, Chris, what would get you to do the dishes anyway, even though there is a crisis and you wouldn't be able to preserve the safety of others?

Chris: If the magnitude of the crisis was beyond my ability to infuence it.

Notice that this response isn't going to a more important criterion, it just makes "preserving safety" irrelevant by changing the existing context. You've turned the crisis into something that you can't have an impact on. What *else* would you have to add to the context we already have so far— few dirty dishes, visiting stranger, cooking a meal, *and* crisis—in order for you to violate "preserving safety?"

Chris: My guess is that I wouldn't do the dishes if there's some way I could help with the crisis.

Right, we have already established that. What would get you to *do* them even though there was some way you could help with the crisis?

Chris: If people more competent than I miraculously appeared to deal with the crisis, then I would do the dishes.

Notice that Chris still isn't going to a higher criterion. He keeps building in a way for his criterion of "preserving safety" to be met. We will know he's going to a higher criterion when he thinks of something *more* important for which he would *sacrifice* "preserving safety." I usually try to get the person to think of something first, before offering a suggestion, but we're close to the top here anyway. Most people value their *own* life over the safety of other people. So, Chris, let's imagine someone had you at gunpoint saying, "If you respond to that crisis, I'll blow your brains out!" Would that get you to do the dishes?

Chris: It might.

It might?! (laughter) What if your family were threatened if you didn't do the dishes?

Chris: I have no immediate family. I live alone. And someone puts a gun to my head at his own risk, so I'm not sure that I would do the dishes even then.

What if you received a phone call that the entire city of New York would be blown up if you didn't do the dishes? You had to do them and ignore the crisis, or New York would be gone.

Chris: OK. . . .

I won't press any further because we're very high now; whether we're at *the* top of his hierarchy or close to it, we're high enough for our purposes. I'm convinced of that on the basis of his response. For some people this wouldn't be the top. For them, the security of others isn't really that important, but if it involves their own lives, they get concerned! And even a person's life might not be as important as his principles, for example, "honor," "doing what's right," or "morality." That's one of the ways that self-sacrifice and war become possible. Chris undoubtedly has many other criteria that would fit between the ones we've elicited here. For our purposes, however, you don't need to elicit every single criterion in order, because you actually only need three for the next step in the exercise: one that's very unimportant, one in the mid-range, and one that's very important. After you have that, we'll demonstrate how to shift a criterion.

Exercise

Get into groups of three, and elicit a hierarchy of criteria from your partner, in the same way I did with Chris. Make sure you start with something really trivial. What is something insignificant she could do, but wouldn't? Her nonverbal response will give you some idea of how trivial or important the behavior is to her. It's important not to superimpose your own criteria on what she's doing. Other people's hierarchies will sometimes be very different from yours, and you need to find out how it is for *this* person. Once your partner has picked a trivial behavior, keep reversing whether she does it or not to elicit successively higher criteria.

The key thing is to keep her going up the hierarchy. Find out what is important enough to get her to sacrifice the last criterion elicited. I asked Chris, "What would get you to do the dishes anyway, *even though* by doing so you would violate the criterion just elicited?'' Then Chris would *add* a new element to the context. I then asked questions to find the criterion that applied in that new context, ''What would doing that *accomplish* for you?'' Then we reversed the question: ''What would get you to *not* do the dishes, even though by not doing them you have to violate this last criterion?''

The chart of Chris's criteria hierarchy given below shows how the context is *cumulative*. At each step we *add* context, but we never subtract any part of what is already there. This is a way to find out what is important enough that it would get Chris to violate the previous criterion.

Behavior	Context	Criterion
(−) Could do dishes, but wouldn't	Few dirty dishes	Save time
(+) Would do dishes	Few dirty dishes *and* Visiting stranger	Neutral impression
(−) Wouldn't do dishes	Few dirty dishes *and* Visiting stranger *and* Cooking meal	Excellence (of cooking)
(+) Would do dishes	Few dirty dishes *and* Visiting stranger *and* Cooking meal *and* Unhygienic dishes	Preserving hygiene
(−) Wouldn't do dishes	Few dirty dishes *and* Visiting stranger *and* Cooking meal *and* Unhygienic dishes *and* Crisis in building.	Preserving others' safety

Man: Could you go for the next criterion by asking, ''Now what's more important than that?''

Yes, but many people will respond, ''Oh, lots of things!'' (laughter) When you ask someone to think so abstractly, he has to guess, but without an appropriate context, he may not be right. By setting up a specific scenario, people are much more likely to identify the criteria that *actually* influence their behavior, in contrast to the criteria they *think* should influence their behavior. The specific scenario makes much better use of unconscious resources, and avoids intellectualization.

Make sure that all criteria are stated in the *positive*. Ask your partner what a criterion preserves or accomplishes, not what it helps her avoid. A good way of discovering this is to ask what a particular behavior does for her. "What makes this of value?" "What are you doing this *for*?"

Sometimes people will give you their criteria slightly out of order, because they're thinking of an experience that violates or satisfies only a little bit of a criterion rather than a lot of it, and this may affect its ordering relative to other criteria. A few dirty dishes doesn't violate "cleanliness" as much as a dismantled car engine in your living room. Once you have a hierarchy, select three criteria that you're pretty certain are in the right order to use for the next step. Pick one trivial, one mid-range, and one important criterion, and check for both verbal and nonverbal congruence. For Chris, I would take "saving time," "excellence," and "preserving safety." These three I'm pretty certain are in the right order, so I can use them.

Next notice how these criteria are represented, and then determine the submodality distinctions that characterize them. If we were doing this with Chris, I'd ask him to think about his criterion "saving time." How does he represent "saving time"? How about "excellence" and "preserving others' safety"? What does he see/hear/feel when he thinks about each of these criteria? Then he can compare these three representations to each other in the same way you compared past, present, and future to discover your timeline. We want you find out which submodalities are used to order these three criteria on a *continuum*. There may also be digital differences, but we're not interested in those right now. We only want analogue submodalities that vary continuously. You may find two or three submodalities that differ, but often one key submodality will be most powerful.

For now, simply *notice* which analogue submodalities seem to be the major way of coding the relative importance of these three criteria. Later, *after* your partner has decided what criterion she would like to shift, you'll test these submodalities. Criteria are surprisingly easy to shift, and we don't want you to shift them accidentally.

If some of you finish early, you can explore the submodality differences between the same criteria stated in the positive in contrast to being stated in the negative.

Man: By stated in the positive, you mean "saving time" rather than "not wasting time?"

Exactly. People move toward positively-stated criteria and away from negatively-stated criteria. If you have some of each, that will confuse you. The submodality codings related to "moving toward" and "moving away from" are interesting, but they are different from how people rank their criteria in a hierarchy. When you delete the effects of "moving toward" and "moving away from" by having all the criteria stated the same way, you have a much better chance of finding *only* the submodalities that relate to the hierarchy itself.

Man: But what about people who are motivated by avoidance rather than by attraction? What if someone's really motivated to avoid things in life?

For some people it may be easier to get all the criteria stated in the negative. Do that only if it really seems difficult to reorient the person toward the positive.

I'd like to enlarge the frame by asking the following question: If someone is truly primarily motivated by avoidance, do you want to leave him with that orientation, or do you want to refocus his attention on what he wants to go towards? Every time you move away from something, you also have to move *toward* something else. If all your attention is on what you're moving away from, you won't notice what you're moving toward. "Out of the frying pan and into the fire" aptly expresses this problem of not noticing what you're moving toward. Focusing this person's attention on what he wants could be far more generative and useful than changing his hierarchy of what to avoid.

There are things in life well worth avoiding. Sometimes it's very good to use "worst-case planning," and some people get into big trouble when they don't. In general, however, well-formed outcomes in NLP are stated in the positive, because you are much more likely to get where you want to go if you orient toward it. This is ground rule number one in practitioner training. *After* you have formulated a positive outcome, *then* you can do "worst-case" planning to be sure you achieve the outcome ecologically.

People occasionally have trouble deciding if something is truly a criterion, or if it's part of the context. The main test to use is that a criterion is a nominalization that can apply in many *different* contexts. One criterion for buying a car may be to have one with bucket seats. That is too specific to go across context, but "physical comfort" or "others' approval" could apply to the car as well as a wide variety of other contexts. You also want to phrase a criterion as concisely as possible; often one or two words will do. One person had the criterion "fitting in with other people." That's a bit long, but it clearly can apply in a wide range of situations and to a wide range of behaviors. That's enough direction for now; go ahead with the exercise.

* * * * *

Discussion

Welcome back! What did you find in there? Some of you are starting to notice fascinating connections. For instance, several groups observed connections between the hierarchy of criteria and the timeline.

Neville: Yes, Tom's timeline and his hierarchy of criteria were exactly the same. What's least important for Tom was in the same location that Tom uses for the past on his timeline, and the more important the criterion was, the more in the future it was. His criteria were arranged along his timeline.

Right. Even without knowing any content, this indicates that he is very future-oriented. I'm similiar to Tom. I tend to ignore the past, so my hierarchy of criteria starts where I represent the present and continues straight into the future. You can expect that a person values the future if he uses the same submodalities to code both future time and highly-valued criteria, as Tom and I do.

In contrast, someone who codes the past and his highly-valued criteria with the same submodalities probably reminisces a lot and would like to go back to the "good old days." "Nostalgia is not what it used to be." (laughter)

Joe: We found it difficult to elicit a criterion for money, because money itself seems to be a measurement of value.

Money is certainly convertible into many things. At the same time, money usually means something fairly specific to the person. You can ask, "What does money get for you? What's important about having money?" For some people money means "security," and that is the value they place on it. For other people, it means "power" or "freedom." What the money is for, what's important or useful about it, will give you the criterion. Once in a while someone does seem to be going for money in and of itself, and has forgotten that he wants the money for something. Misers do that; they save money but never use it. Once in a while money seems to be the person's key criterion in and of itself: "It's just money, that's all I want." If so, it's time to redirect him toward his outcomes.

Bill: Connirae, since your timeline and your value system are so closely correlated, does the criterion associated with the present on the time line somehow take precedence over your other values?

No, not for me. My behavior *now* is motivated much more by the future, and more by the long-range future than by the immediate future; I will put up with present difficulties in order to get long-term results.

Many of you noticed a location sort for the hierarchy of criteria. Your criteria are arranged in space, either up to down, near to far, left to right, etc. Lots of us talk about our criteria as "highly"-valued, and we very literally arrange our hierarchies that way; certain criteria are higher, others are lower. However, some people reverse this: lower is more important. These people are more apt to talk about "fundamental" or "basic" values.

Rita used closeness; certain values were more "at the forefront" for her than others, and she talked about them as being "closely-held" values. Another person ranked her criteria by size. Everything was in the same location, but the *bigger* the picture, the more she valued it.

Carol: I seem to be an exception. My timeline goes from left to right, but all my criteria are straight ahead.

Are they all in the same spot, or do they go out into the distance?

Carol: They're all in the same spot.

How can you tell one is more important than another, then?

Carol: My less important criterion is like a flat sheet of paper. The one in the middle is an associated color movie, and my important one is straight auditory—I don't get pictures for it at all.

It sounds like these three criteria have no submodalities in common. In order to have a *hierarchy*, you need to have submodalities in some kind of continuum. Some people have only two digital categories: something is either *important* or it's *not*. "Black-and-white," "right-or-wrong" thinkers often structure their experience in either/or digital categories. Other people may have three or more categories. I encountered one woman who had only three levels of criteria. Decision-making was very easy for her, because all the criteria at the same level were equally important; if she had a choice between alternatives that satisfied two different criteria at the same level, she simply chose one at random.

It's possible that Carol has only three digital categories of how important something could be, but she doesn't seem like that kind of person, so I'm skeptical. Carol, here's something to try out on your own. Take those three criteria and make sure that they are all in the same representational system. In order to find the submodality that varies along a continuum, your criteria all need to be represented in the same system. You can't have a continuum if they skip from auditory to visual and so forth. You may actually have one way of ordering your criteria auditorily and another way of doing it visually, but for this exercise, don't mix up the two systems.

Bob: We started trying to find visual submodalities for each criterion, and it got very confusing. We couldn't find anything, so we decided to drop that and go to auditory. We also used vague hypnotic language, like "Get a sense of this experience." He did get auditory differences, and he demonstrated them for us in his voice and tempo. But he also had a very definite continuum with his direction of gaze from top to bottom, whenever he was not concentrating on the pictures.

Great. Nice observation. So you ended up with a nice hierarchy, even though he wasn't conscious of it. Always keep your eyes and ears open.

Tom: We were amazed by the congruence between the location of criteria and the verbal language and body language used to describe them.

Yes. You can use that information in two powerful ways: you can covertly identify how someone orders criteria, and you can also use body language to make it easier for someone to adjust his criteria, which is the next step.

Selecting a Criterion Worth Changing

Now that you've all identified what submodalities let your brain know which criteria are more or less important to you, the next step is to use that information to adjust a criterion that you feel is out of place.

People have done some very worthwhile things with this pattern; let me give you a few examples. One clinical psychologist made an important shift in his relationship with his wife. He had found himself constantly correcting her trivial mistakes. She'd say, "Well, last Wednesday when we went to the movies . . . " and he'd say, "No, it was Thursday." When he did this, he'd realize that he was being obnoxious and unnecessarily annoying his wife, but the corrections would just pop out of his mouth! He recognized the harm that he was doing, but he couldn't change it. So much for conscious insight.

When he explored his criteria, he discovered that he was responding to his highly-valued criterion of "correctness." He wanted his wife to be right. Of course by correcting her he was making her *wrong*, but that's often how these things work! His representation of wanting her to be right was a picture of a pointing finger, which he made less important by moving it downward. As the picture moved down, it spontaneously whited out and transformed into a picture of figures dancing. His whole posture softened at that point, and tears came to his eyes. The representation of the criterion itself had spontaneously changed to an entirely different content. He was amazed at how much differently he felt toward his wife when he thought about her making a mistake.

I've done a number of criteria shifts on myself. For example, once I was about to go to Boston to teach a seminar, and I felt the signs of a cold or the flu coming on. I knew I was getting sick, and I also knew that it wouldn't do to get sick right then. I initially attempted to do a little reframing. I went inside and tried promising my body: "All right, I'll take a break as soon as I get back—I just need these four days to do this seminar. Leave me in peace and then I will rest." (laughter) This approach has worked in the past, but I knew it wasn't working in this case because I wasn't getting any response from my body.

When I checked for the objection—what stopped me from being well— what came up was the importance of my relationship with Steve. We had tons of things to do; it was important to him to get them all done, and I wanted to do my part. It was only *my* perception that he wanted me to work on all these things rather than rest. In fact, he probably would have encouraged me to take it easy and keep my health. However, unconsciously the way I thought about it was that my relationship with Steve was more important than my physical health, so the promise to rest if my body would stay healthy for the Boston seminar was in conflict with my desire to work hard to get things done when I got back. With this information, I went inside and shifted the importance of my own physical health, making that *more* important than my relationship with Steve. I had a different physical response then and immediately knew that I would be well.

Man: Was this criterion shift temporary, only until you finished your workshop?

No, it was permanent. I thought it was a good idea that my physical health always be more important. Being healthy actually makes my relationship with Steve better in the long run. You can't have a very good relationship with someone if you're sick, or if you work so hard you die young. So that's another example of how a criterion shift can be useful.

Now let's consider the following situation. For one participant "being right" was a highly-valued criterion that got him into trouble. He found himself constantly attempting to prove how smart he was, and demonstrating that he was right about things. At the same time, he recognized that this created problems for him, so he decided to adjust the importance of "being right" to make it less important.

When you do a criterion shift, you can either adjust *one* criterion, or you can simultaneously make one criterion less important as you make another one more important. This is particularly important when the person perceives another criterion as a complementary opposite. For example, many people perceive "pleasing others" in balance with "pleasing myself." Since just taking something away is often not ecologically sound, what might we want to make more important when we make "being right" less important for this person?

Man: "Being helpful."

That's a possibility. You could have the person think about the impor-tance of "being right," and get a representation of that. Then have him move the representation down, or farther away, or make it smaller, or whatever makes it less important, at the same time that he moves "being helpful" up. That might work for some people. What else might work?

Man: "Being right" sounds like he needs external approval about his behavior. What if he switched to knowing internally that he was right, without needing feedback from other people?

I think you're on the right track. One possible danger is that he could end up "knowing" he's right and not being open to external feedback when he's actually wrong.

Woman: How about replacing "being right" with "having balanced relationships?"

So rather than needing to control a situation by being right, it would be more important to cooperate with other people—have symmetrical relationships.

Man: How about "being loved" versus "being right?"

That's a possibility, although "being loved" also emphasizes the need to get responses from other people. That could keep the client in a very vulnerable position. What else might you do? What most of you are doing intuitively is to think about a different *outcome* that might be useful for him. One way to get this would be to ask him, "What does being right get for you?" This might give us a criterion to use in place of being right. Or, we can ask him what *he* wants to have as more important.

Woman: How about replacing "being right" with "being congenial?"

Yes, or maybe "getting responses from others," or "having an impact in a graceful way." Or he might decrease the importance of needing to *prove* he is right. When someone spends time *proving* he is right, he is less apt to be right, because he's so busy spending time trying to prove it.

Man: "Being right" seems like a state and "proving you're right" seems like a process. So how about substituting a different process?

So instead of having to prove that he's right, he could focus on the importance of learning—or even learning enjoyably. Sometimes you can add criteria like "fun," "enjoyment," and "excitement" to the main criterion you're adjusting.

There are *lots* of things that could go in the place of "being right." When you help other people adjust criteria, be careful not to impose what *you* think is important on the whole world. Sometimes a person comes to you with an outcome and you think, "Wow, that's not very worthwhile!" When that happens, keep in mind that the criteria shift is for helping people adjust *their* own criteria to get more of what *they* want in life. They may want to be very different than you want to be. As long as the change doesn't violate your ethics, and is congruent with their other outcomes and criteria, help them make it.

When I work with someone, I don't attempt to prescribe what she should put in place of a particular criterion. I make suggestions and comments to help her find out what is ecological for her, and I discuss ecology problems. For example, if she chooses "being loved," I'll say, "Well, do you really want to be so much at the mercy of other people's behavior?" She may then want to go for something else. There's no one right answer, because the right answer will be determined by the person who wants to change. If you raise lots of possibilities, you can notice what the person responds to. The elements we've discussed give you some ways of helping the client make a truly appropriate change.

Criteria Shift Demonstration

(The following transcript is taken from a training Connirae did in Dallas, Texas, in January 1986. This demonstration is also in videotape form: see Appendix I. The transcript has been minimally edited for easier reading.)

Do you want to see me demonstrate the change piece quickly? OK. Who has their hierarchy sorted out, number one? And number two, you know something that either you want to make more important, or less important. In thinking about this, think about all the information you have personally, and think about what other people have told you. Is there something that other people think you could make more or less important? This doesn't mean you *should*, but it is a source of information. You can consider it, and decide if *you* think it is a good idea or not.

David (briskly): OK. What do you need?

This man has efficiency in getting down to business! OK, what is your hierarchy? How do you code it submodalities-wise?

David: Submodalities-wise, I have "enjoyment," (gesturing with his left hand toward the distance, slightly to his left). Then "personal improvement" (gesturing about 2 feet straight in front), and then "family" (gesturing with both hands close to his chest) and I'm in it.

And which is more important?

David: Family.

OK, I suspected this. So he has "closely-held" criteria. I always talk about "highly-valued" criteria, and that is a really common way of speaking about criteria. Some people have closely-held criteria, and other people have "basic" values. OK, so his criteria are in a line slightly off to the left with one criterion in the distance, and the more important ones closer. Now do you have something in mind that you want to make more important or less important?

David: Uh-huh.

Do you want to tell us or not? You don't have to. It doesn't matter.

David: Well, I've got a problem here. When you were talking a while ago, it connected with something that has been churning for a while. I will let myself go to the point of being sick, working myself to death, before taking care of personal needs. I need to bring that *up* (gesturing toward chest with both hands) in importance.

"Taking care of personal needs." (Right.) OK. Now, you want to get some idea of where the person wants this criterion to end up, otherwise you may have it come in more important than life itself before you realize, "Hey wait a minute, not *that* important." So, what do you want it to be as important as, or more important than?

David: More important than working myself to death.

Good choice. (laughter) No argument from me.

David: Well, I have a hard time with the work setting, saying "No." I can be just ready-for-bed sick, and I'll go ahead and go.

OK. Now we'll do an ecology check. It sounds good, basically. I want to make sure that the way *he* interprets it will work out well for him. So, if you imagine that you had responding to personal needs more important than work, and accomplishing things and so on, . . . imagine how your life would be different. And just check. Are there any problems with life that way? . . .

David: Hmm. It is going to be very *different*. It's sort of like there's a part that's going, "What *will* it be like?"

"I wonder." Yes, so you may not know fully, and that may mean that later on, after we have done this change, that you end up wanting to adapt it a little, which is fine. You can go right back in and adapt it; you might have to add something in or take something out, or move it.

David: Well, the thing that keeps coming up is just the whole nature of efficiency. If I take better care of myself I will be more efficient in the work setting anyway.

That's true. So they don't really conflict. (Right.) Now when you think about taking care of personal needs, where do you see that right now?

David: Right out there. (He points straight ahead and up with right hand.) *Way* out there (both hands).

Way out there, OK. This is a clue. Is it in line with your other criteria or is it off the line?

David: Uh, it's pretty much center, and up, and—

What I mean is, is it in line—

David: —it is about as far out as Allen is, (Allen is seated in the back of the room.) but up about ceiling level.

I see what you mean about bringing this in! (Allen raises both hands.)

David: Thanks! (He waves to Allen, and gives him the OK sign.)

Allen, would you just move in when I give you the cue? (joking)

David: Hold your hands up and bring it to me. (laughter)

OK. Now where is "responding to working?"

David: OK. Working. Kind of off down there. (He points straight ahead and down, slightly to the right.)

And how far away?

David: Just this side of the TV. Just right down there.

Down by the TV. OK, now let's test a little bit. These two criteria are in a different location than the first three; it's not just a straight line. I want to test to find out if up and down matters. So take the one about work. (OK) If you move it up slightly—we're going to put this back—but if you move it up (David shakes his head) temporarily, does it seem more or less important?

David: (His hand moves left and right in direction of the work criterion.) There's a very—it's going . . . (He laughs and gestures out and up away from him with his right hand) it is going out as it's coming up (gestures toward the "personal needs" criterion). It's just kind of there.

Oh! So it is on a trajectory with that other criterion. OK. Put it back. (OK.) Now what I would like you to do is take the one for responding to personal needs—(Allen raises his hands, and David laughs and points to Allen) This is your cue, Allen! . . . And now I want you to move this criterion in closer. This technique you do slowly—you don't do it quickly— so that you can notice the impact as you are moving it in. And you can kind of check internally. Usually people get a sense of when the criterion is in the right place. You also have a target destination. You know you would like it to be more important than working. So let the picture gradually move in, and you can notice the impact that it has, as it becomes more important, and just get a feel for when it is in the right place. . . . (David makes a questioning sound.) Eeh-eah. (He rocks his left hand for "iffy" or unsure.)

Move it back and forth a little bit if you are not quite sure. Test it out.
David: Oh, if I move it in further, OK.

Good. And one of the interesting phenomena that seems to happen as you do this is that when it gets in the right spot, it kind of plunks in— (David nods his head, "Yes," and both hands gesture "Of course")— particularly if you tell people that it will. (laughter) (David's hands move as if setting something in place.) It just kind of settles in there, . . . gets in the right spot. The "plunk" technique. OK, and let me know when it seems to be settling in the right spot.

David: OK. Sort of. ("Sort of"?) Well, you know I'm not used to (He moves his body back) it being that close. It's sort of like, "Huh" . . . (hand on chin in "thoughtful" position). I'm noticing several other things about it, too.

Do you notice anything that you might want to adjust? You can probably see it more clearly up here. You might not have been sure what was in that picture when it was farther away.

David: That's what I'm noticing.

You may want to shift the content a little bit now that it's come in closer and you can see what is in there. . . .

David: Hmmn. . . . Yeah, it is extremely complex.

Is that good or . . . ?

David: Surprising.

OK. Complex in what way?

David: Well, when I was thinking in the "personal need" ballpark, I was thinking of physical illness, and yet that seems to be a minute part of it. (His left thumb and one finger make a small pointing gesture.) You know, it's . . . (His left hand draws a larger circle in space around the previous gesture.)

Some part of your brain stuck a whole bunch of things in there—

David: Yeah, because the content, you know, like physical health (That's one piece, OK.) is just down in this little— (Both index fingers trace a small rectangle in the center of the circle.)

Then what I want you to do is check the other pieces of it that you didn't realize were there, and make sure that you are happy with them being in this place of importance.

David: OK, when you said that it started shuffling stuff around.

Good. There may be pieces of that picture that you want to move back farther, or there may be pieces that want to come in even closer. . . .

David: (nodding) They did. OK. That's neat. OK.

Good. Looking at the configuration now, is this one that you think will work for you? Or are there any other further adjustments?

David: It seems that something is not exactly right—like it is just real close, but not quite there.

OK, so take your time so that it can begin to stand out to you. Just sort of scan the whole thing.

David: (laughs) Hi Allen! You're not quite there, but, . . . I'll use your right shoulder for a corner of it. . . . OK (closes eyes)

And as you are doing that, I will say a few things to the group that you already know. . . . What I want to comment on is that as you do this kind of a process, if you incorporate hypnotic language patterns it makes it much easier for the person. You say things like, "You can *allow* that image to come closer, and *notice* when it finds the right spot," (David nods) so that you presuppose certain things that you don't want to call into question, which would make it more difficult than necessary for a person. That's a lot easier than saying, "Does it have a right spot?" because then they'll start wondering. . . . l

David: OK. As I have allowed it to work, the screen has expanded (He draws a large rectangle in front of him with both hands.) out there to be a big rectangle, with chunks through it. (He makes choppy vertical hand movements from left to right). . . . So it is like—(His right hand sweeps from left to right in front of him, as he whistles softly.)

So it is spread out.

David: Yeah. It's kind of neat.

Did that seem—

David: Yeah, after I let it kind of—(expands arms outward). . . .

Expand. (Uh-huh.) And that makes sense, so that you can really see it fully and know what's there.

David: (nodding) Uh-huh. And I am getting all kinds of strange kinesthetics now (Both hands rotate in alternating circles near stomach.), kind of like "Wow!" (His head and chest move back.)

And the only thing to check for is, are the "strange kinesthetics" strange as in "This is different, I haven't been this way before." (David is nodding, "Uh-huh") Because if they are the "something is wrong" kind of kinesthetics, then you would want to make further adjustments. And David is congruently responding to "This is just unfamiliar." OK. That's the change part.

Now what we want to do is test. (OK.) This particular change is a little more difficult to test than some. If you can create something behaviorally on the spot, test it that way. For example, one person lowered the importance of other people's opinions, and increased the importance of doing what he thought was right. Immediately afterwards someone in his group told him to do something, "Do this with your submodalities," and his instant response was, "No, I don't think that is the right thing. I need to do something else." It was an unintended move, but they realized in retrospect that it served as a great test. So that is one way you can test sometimes. We can't do that with this particular change, but we can always test in imagination. Imagine yourself in a setting where this will make a difference. (He closes his eyes.) It's the most general test you can do. Have them pick a context where this new configuration will make a difference. . . .

David: (He nods and smiles, very relaxed.) OK, I've got it.

What do you think? Looks good to me.

David: "No" came out real easy. It was a typical phone call of somebody, "I need you now," and a real quick check, "No, you can call so-and-so." (He snaps his fingers.)

Great. Yeah, and it is that kind of automatic shift that you get when people's criteria are in a different alignment. You don't have to *make* yourself act differently, it is just the way you are. OK, try another context, I like to be thorough in my testing. (He closes his eyes. "OK. Another context.") Another context where having this new configuration will make a difference. . . . (OK.)

How is that one?

David: Surprising. (laughter)

Is it surprising and delightful, or . . . ?

David: Yeah, it is. I took the alternative where somebody gave me the opportunity to go do something just for me. And typically I would refuse those and say, "No, I don't have time." And I was going with it and I thought, "What am I doing?" (Head looks around in a circle) "This is not normal." So, that's kind of nice.

OK, good. And if you can think of yet a third context. . . . Three is a magic number in NLP. . . .

David: (He tilts his head up to his right) Boy, that is one that I haven't seen in a long time. (laughter) I mean, face it, it has been seven years since I've had a vacation.

You're worse than we are! . . .

David: That is neat. It just got written into my calendar.

OK, this looks good to me, and three satisfies my criteria for a good test. So thank you.

David: Thank you.

Now, one of the things I would be careful about in making a maneuver like this is to make sure he doesn't go too far in the direction of, "Now he is going to go on vacation 300 days of the year and work 65." (laughter) I didn't get any indication from him that he would go that far. He is going,

"I am writing a vacation on my calendar, but I haven't had a vacation in seven years." It is not like, "I am going to take five years off." Then I would start wondering, "What have I done here?" So you might test the limits a little bit after you make a shift with someone, to make sure they haven't gone too far. If he stops work, and the money stops coming in, he is going to have trouble going on vacation.

Criteria Shift Exercise

Let's go over the steps of the criteria shift briefly, and then you can do it.

1. First take the submodality codings you've already elicited, and identify how they create a continuum. With David, the most important submodality was distance: the more important the criterion, the closer it was to him.

2. Help your partner identify a criterion she wants to make more or less important, and find out where this criterion is on her hierarchy of criteria. Be sure to check for ecology.

3. After you've identified the criterion your partner is going to shift, determine where she wants it to end up. Does she want to make it *more* important, *as* important, or *less* important than some other criterion? Find out where this second criterion is in the hierarchy.

4. Next slowly change the criterion in the appropriate way (closeness, size, brightness, color, etc.). Adjust submodalities so that the criterion is coded for the degree of importance the person wants it to have. For example, if being higher up makes something more important, and your partner wants to make something more important, have your partner take the representation of that criterion and allow it to rise slowly until it finds the right spot. If she sorts by size, she can allow the picture to enlarge slowly until it's just the right size to let her know it's as important as she wants it to be. If she's sorting by auditory volume, she can let the sound get louder until it's at just the right level.

Even if a person hasn't identified what he wants the new criterion to be more or less important than, when you ask him to move it to the "right spot," he will usually have a good intuition for where that is. People have also reported that if they move the new criterion too fast, they know right away that it's going too far, and they move it back down to where they feel more comfortable. They can feel when it's out of place, and that feeling usually signals an ecology concern.

Keep in mind that this is a change to do slowly. You can use hand gestures to help your client, but don't go farther or faster than she does.

If she's raising a criterion, don't quickly zoom it up and make it more important than life itself. If you do this too quickly, "being tidy" could end up more important than "staying alive"! (laughter) This is not ecological!

When you ask the person to "bring a criterion closer," it is coming closer *in relationship to the other things on their hierarchy of criteria.* That's what makes this work. Sometimes I add to my preliminary instructions, "OK, now you can have the sense that all your other criteria are also there and a part of that continuum." You'll get more experience of how all this works when you do the exercise.

Testing

There are several possible ways for you to test your work. The first way is to pause and do something else for a little while. Then ask the client to think about the criterion she shifted. How does she experience it now? Is it naturally where she wants it to be? Is it high enough, or close enough, or enough of whatever she used to change it?

The second way of testing is especially important, because it's also a future-pace. Ask her to think of a situation where the new criterion will make a difference for her, and then put her into that context and find out what her experience is. Is it what she wants? This is the kind of test that I did with David. With either test of course, you watch for nonverbal confirmation that the intervention has made a difference. If you have any doubts, or you want to be very thorough, test in several contexts.

A third possibility is to set up a behavioral test. Create a situation in which you expect that the criteria shift will make a difference, and notice what happens.

All right, go ahead and do this. We'll discuss it afterwards.

Exercise Summary

1. Identify the major submodality that creates a continuum for the hierachy of criteria.
2. Identify a criterion to adjust, and its present location on the continuum.
3. Determine a general target location on the continuum.
4. Slowly adjust the criterion in the direction of the target location until it feels right.

Discussion

Congratulations! I've noticed that a *lot* of you were doing very nice things with this. Let's hear a few testimonials. (laughter) David told me he realized his mind was continuing to do more reshuffling and more adjustment to align the change we did in a more purposeful conscious way up here.

David: I'm still checking it out. Things are reshuffling all over the place. And the change is remaining congruent with my timeline, in both directions. I have a timeline belt that goes past (gesturing to his left) and future (gesturing to his right). And then my day goes top to bottom, and everything is falling into place along the continuum.

Good. It's nice to be aware of that kind of continuing reshuffling. If you make this shift with yourself or with someone else, either allow time for furthur adjustments—don't immediately go off to another activity that would be incongruent—or make arrangements to let it happen at the unconscious level, as David is doing. Make sure that the conscious mind can be available and alert for whatever you are about to undertake.

Leah: After we determined everyone's continuum in our group, we each decided what criterion we wanted to change, and in which direction. Then we each instructed our unconscious minds to make the appropriate adjustments for us. We tested later, and it worked great.

That's a nice adaption.

Ben: My least important criterion was close in front of me and the most important one was far away! I'd respond to what was close even though that was trivial, and I didn't respond to what was actually important to me off in the distance! When I realized that, I said to myself, "That's nuts " and switched the whole thing around.

And that really changed his state I was sitting in on Ben's group earlier. Do you all understand what he did? Rather than simply changing the position of a criterion within the stack, he. shifted the whole stack around, so that it is congruent with what he wants his brain to recognize as important. What is important is now close, and the trivial criteria are farther away. That's great!

Ben: I think I know how it got set up that way, too. I had an experience a long time ago that I didn't like, which made me turn all my criteria around.

When Ben told me this earlier, I asked him to check for ecology before shifting his criteria. I wanted him to check whether something about his previous arrangement had *produced* that unpleasant experience, in which case it wouldn't be ecological to change them back.

Ben: And that's not the case at all. They'll be fine the way they are now.

Let me tell you about an interesting example. Chris made "having to be right" less important, and without advance planning, "humor" popped up to take its place. I thought that was very nice. Humor is great, and many of us could make useful changes by increasing its importance in our lives.

Fred: I was shifting the importance of "flexibility." When I started to make it more important, "flexibility" started to ripple through the whole system, all the way down to the bottom of my hierarchy. Suddenly I got flexibility in *all* these different places.

So you built flexibility into many different criteria. Very nice. That's similar to what a group over here did with "fun." It's an interesting variation: not simply changing a criterion, but letting it flow through and affect the entire hierarchy.

David: We utilized the correlation between criteria and the timeline in our group. If Tim wanted something more important, he moved it over here in the future, and it automatically fell into a slot. If he wanted something to be less important, he moved it over to the past.

Bill: When I did this, I made eating carrots more important, and I got a "should." I felt like I "should" eat carrots, and that it was really important, but I didn't like it.

Eating carrots is a *behavior*, not a criterion. What's important to you about eating carrots? Is it something like health, or fitness? (Yes.) So, you might think about making your overall health more important. That's the criterion. When you try that out my guess is that you won't get a "should."

I noticed that several of you were trying to make a specific behavior more important, rather than identifying the general criterion it satisfies and making *that* more important. A behavior is specific and contextualized, like eating carrots, or doing more homework. The value of identifying and changing a criterion is that you get a shift that will affect the person across contexts, and you have more freedom to choose specific behaviors that satisfy the criterion.

You can think about what level of generalization you want to work on. If you only want to change a specific behavior, preserving ecology is relatively easy. Criteria, however, are at the next higher level of generalization. Since they go across contexts, making a change at the level of criteria will have a more pervasive impact. Because of this, you need to be more careful to check the ecology of a criterion shift.

You can also future-pace a criterion shift *only* into certain contexts. If I want a criterion shifted only when I work with clients, for example, I can imagine that I am in that context, and do the criteria shift against the background of that context. Then, to be sure the criterion shift hasn't overgeneralized, I can imagine that I am in another context and check my criteria to be sure they are in the order I want them in there. You generalize a new criterion the same way that you generalize any other change: imagine applying the new criterion in all the different contexts where it would be useful, and *not* in others.

Mary: How will I know when to use this method?

It takes more sensitivity on your part to determine when to make a criterion shift. When a client comes in with a complaint, he doesn't usually say, "I have this criterion that I need to make less important." He usually complains about feeling bad in some way. As you gather information, you may notice a theme. You may notice that in many ways he is not taking his health seriously enough, or that it's too important for him to be right, or in control. Seeing a pattern across contexts is an indication that changing a criterion can be useful.

One way to think about this is to gather information and ask yourself, "What are the relevant criteria?" "What would happen if some of these were more important or less important? Would that be useful for this person in relation to his problem?"

We're being very picky about details in all the exercises in this training—having you get precise information about lots of submodalities, testing them thoroughly, and so on. We think this is valuable background experience, because it allows you to get a full representation in your mind about how these patterns work. Once you've had some practice gathering in-depth information, you usually won't need to get that kind of detail with clients in order to help them change.

A simpler (but less sure) way to do this with a client is to ask, "What is something trivial? What is something of medium importance? What is something of great importance to you?" Then get the criteria and notice how he represents those criteria.

Often I simply ask a person to think of something very important, and as he accesses it, I watch his nonverbal cues. Then I ask him to think of something trivial, and watch again. A person will almost always look in two different spots, and that's all I need. Since most people have a location sort for their hierarchy of criteria, I can check that out quickly and not have to spend a half-hour gathering detailed information.

You can do all these patterns "quick and dirty" in the real world, after you become familiar with them. If you run into difficulty, you can always back up and gather more detailed information. However, if you *start* learning these patterns by doing them "quick and dirty," your work will end up being sloppy and ineffective instead of precise and fast. Going through a pattern very carefully at least a few times is an extremely valuable experience that keeps your work clean and systematic.

Positive vs. Negative Criteria

Did any of you have time to explore the difference between person is going towards versus what he is going away from? Let's quickly play with this as a group. Think about several of your positive criteria, the things you're moving towards, such as "learning," "happiness," "personal safety," or "preserving life." Notice the submodalities of those representations. . . . Now contrast that with representations of the same criteria stated negatively as something to avoid: "ignorance," "misery," "danger," "death." What are the submodality differences between these two sets of pictures? Which is more fun to look at? The first set, right?

Joe: The things I'm moving toward are brighter, more colorful, three-dimensional. And they're movies rather than slides.

Is that fairly consistent with the rest of you? Many of you are nodding. All of these distinctions tend to go with representations of what you're moving towards. The positive colorful, three-dimensional, and have more movement. On the other hand, criteria stated in the negative—what your're avoiding or moving away from—tend to be dim, still, less colorful, etc. Often they are stark black and white pictures, without any analogue gradations. When people feel threatened, they literally resort to rigid, "black-and-white" ways of thinking, and lose the ability to think of things in terms of a continuum. Most of their thinking resources, such as considering other alternatives, or noticing variations on a continuum, simply aren't available to them until they feel safer.

When you're actually in mortal danger and have to act fast, it's useful to have your brain present you with very simple black-and-white choices. However, when you're not in danger, this kind of thinking is severely limiting.

This is one reason why it makes sense to state well-formed outcomes in the positive. Think how profoundly you change a person's internal experience when you do nothing more than use the outcome frame to focus on what she wants, what she's moving toward, rather than what she's moving away from and doesn't want.

Discovering these relationships between positively- and negatively-stated criteria and their submodality distinctions was interesting to us. As you apply the criteria shift in your own and others' lives, we hope you'll discover other useful distinctions to add to your appreciation of this useful pattern.

V

Eliminating Compulsions

Most people have some behavior or feeling that they *have to have* in a given context. For instance, some people *have to* straighten a crooked picture hanging on the wall. They *can't* leave it crooked and feel fine, even if it's someone else's picture in someone else's house. Some people feel compelled to eat chocolate; they *can't not* eat it if it's around. And if it's not around, they may have to go out and buy some! Other people have to eat ice cream, or potato chips. Some people have to pick up a penny when they see one in the street, or they have to check every pay phone for change. Some people are compelled to read the entire newspaper, even if they don't want to.

Most of these compulsions are fairly trivial, although any eating compulsion *can* have significant consequences. What we call "the compulsion blowout" allows you to eliminate even very intense, strong compulsions—often in minutes—so it's a very powerful pattern. We want you to try it out on a trivial compulsion first. Then, when you have learned the method, you can apply it to more significant behaviors and responses that make a lot more difference to you. The compulsion blowout is perfect for behaviors or responses that are too intense to eliminate easily with other techniques such as the swish pattern.

After you break a compulsion you will still be *able* to do that behavior; you just won't be *compelled* to do it. If you break your compulsion to eat chocolates, you'll still be able to eat them, you just won't feel driven to. Once we demonstrated this method with someone who wanted to eliminate his compulsion to respond to all his phone call messages immediately. Afterwards, he still returned most phone calls soon, he just didn't get high blood pressure over postponing a call that was less important.

89

You can also use this pattern to eliminate compulsions to get angry or violent. However, don't pick a response that involves violence when you're first learning this pattern. It's important to really know what you're doing before you use it for something like that.

Demonstration: Eliciting Submodality Drivers
We're going to demonstrate first, and then discuss how and when to use this method in an ecological way. For the demonstration, and also for the exercise that follows, we want you to pick a fairly trivial compulsion; something that really pulls on you, but if you got rid of this behavior, you wouldn't miss it.

First we will quickly demonstrate how to elicit the submodalities that drive the compulsion. After you have all done that in an exercise, we'll go on to demonstrate how to use them to eliminate the compulsion. Who wants to find out how your compulsion works?

OK, Rachel, what are you compelled to do?

Rachel: I have to eat chocolate kisses. I get really attracted to them.

What's something similar that you feel neutral about?

Rachel: I'm not particularly attracted to cookies. I can take them or leave them.

Great. And you won't mind if this compulsion gets broken, right?

Rachel: Not at all.

Good. Now, I want you to think about chocolate kisses, and notice how they look when you think of them. . . . And then think about cookies; notice what they look like in your mind. . . .

Now check for submodality differences. What's different about the way you see chocolate kisses in contrast to the way you see cookies?

Rachel: The chocolate kisses seem a little closer. They almost leap off the plate. I guess it's not that the whole picture is closer, just the kisses. The cookies don't do that.

Good. What other differences do you notice?

Rachel: The chocolate kisses are brighter, too, and they almost have a halo around them. That's all I notice.

Is there any difference in how things sound to you?

Rachel: No. I don't hear anything in either one.

Are there any differences in the kinesthetic system *other than* the feeling of compulsion?

Rachel: Well, I feel pulled toward them.

That's part of your response: the feeling of compulsion. We're only interested in discovering any kinesthetic sensations that might help *create* that response.

Now we have several differences in submodalities, so we have some idea of how Rachel's brain codes "I have to have something." In this case, they are all visual. By coding her images in a certain way, Rachel's brain knows instantly, just by looking at the image, which things she has to have, like kisses, and which things she has choice about, like cookies.

The next step is to test, to find out which of these submodality differences is the most important "driver" that creates her compulsive response.

Rachel, take a look at the image of the chocolate kisses. Try making the kisses a little bit closer. Make them leap off the plate a little bit more. Does this make you feel more or less compelled to eat the chocolates?

Rachel: (Her skin gains color, and she makes mouth movements.) Yes, right away I want them more.

OK. Now move the kisses back onto the plate. Does this change your response?

Rachel: That makes me not want them so much.

Now let's try changing the brightness. Make the chocolate kisses a little brighter. Does this change your response?

Rachel: It does, but not as much. I think that when I made the kisses leap out more, they got a little brighter at the same time. If I just make them brighter, I don't feel much different.

So this indicates that the closeness is a driver submodality; it drives Rachel's response, and changes the brightness as well. Let's test a bit further. Try intensifying the halo. . . .

Rachel: That makes me want it more—but not as much as making the chocolates leap out farther.

Try reducing the halo. . . .

Rachel: It makes me respond a little less to the kisses, but I still want them.

Now we know that the key submodality that "drives" Rachel's response is having the image leap out toward her, and away from the background.

Exercise

Next we want you all to do this much with each other. This is as far as we want you to go at this point. Be sure to pick a compulsion that you won't mind losing, because after the exercise you probably won't have it anymore. You might ask yourself, "Would my life be missing anything without this compulsion?" Since you're going to be rid of it, we want to be sure you'll be better off.

When you've thought of your compulsion, think of a similar behavior that you're *not* compelled to do. If you *have to* read all the comics, maybe you don't have to read all of the sports page. If you're compelled to drink coffee, perhaps you don't have to drink tea—you can take it or leave it. If you're overly compelled to wash every dish in the kitchen, perhaps you're not compelled to sweep the floors. The more similar the two behaviors are, the better.

Be sure that you pick something *neutral* for the noncompulsive behavior. Do *not* pick something that *repels* you, because repulsion and attraction are actually very similar. They are both forms of compulsion; only the *direction* of the compulsion is different: away, instead of toward. If you are compelled to eat chocolate, pick some food you could eat, but don't feel you *have to* eat. Don't pick some food that disgusts you.

When you have those two experiences—compulsive versus neutral—do a contrastive analysis. What are the differences in submodalities, and which submodality drives the compulsion? Be sure to check all representational systems. Discover the difference that makes a difference.

There are several ways to test which submodalities are the drivers. We could have had Rachel look at the cookies, the neutral experience, and start making them leap out. We could find out if this makes her feel compelled to eat cookies. If you test in that way, make sure the person changes each submodality only a little bit, and fairly slowly. If he goes too fast, you may install another compulsion! It's a little safer to test by changing the compulsion experience itself, as we demonstrated. Test each submodality difference between the neutral experience and the compulsion experience. It's a good idea to test both ways—have the person make the picture brighter, . . . and then dimmer.

Helen: Are we looking for a single submodality?

With compulsions, usually one submodality drives the others. If you find two drivers, that's fine.

Be sure to find an *analogue* submodality that drives the compulsion—one that you can vary continuously over a range. A digital submodality won't work for this pattern. We'll discuss this in more detail later.

After you have identified the submodality differences and tested to find the driver(s), we want you to do one more thing, which we didn't demonstrate. Find out if you can eliminate the compulsion by simply *reducing* the driver. Let's say you discover that the driving submodality for your partner is size; when the ice cream gets bigger, she wants it more. I want you to find out if you can get rid of this compulsion just by making the ice cream look smaller. You already know that this reduced your partner's feeling of compulsion temporarily when you tested it. The question is whether you can *permanently* eliminate her compulsion this way. Ask your partner to see the ice cream get smaller, until she can look at the ice cream and say, "No, I'm not attracted to it now," or "I could have it, but I don't have to." Then, after talking about something else for a few minutes, test again. Have her think about the ice cream, and find out if she feels compelled to have it, or if she still feels neutral. We want you to find out if simply decreasing the driving submodality will eliminate the compulsion.

Take about ten minutes each to do this exercise, and then come back for the next step.

Exercise Outline
1. Think of a minor compulsion.
2. Think of something similar to which you have a neutral response.
3. Identify submodality differences.
4. Test to find the most powerful "driver" submodality.

*   *   *   *   *

Discussion
Tom: I was working with Bob, and when I asked him about submodality differences, he said he didn't notice any.

If your partner doesn't notice the differences, there are several other ways to discover the important submodalities. You can ask, "What do you have to do to the picture of the compulsion to make you want it *more*?" The person will often just tell you: "If I make it bigger, I want it more."

Another way is to have him try to *resist* his compulsion. Set the scene first. If it's chocolates, you can say, "Imagine a plate of chocolates right there in front of you. Now turn and walk away. . . . What happens? Do you want the chocolates more? How do you know you want them more?" Usually he will feel increased desire as he walks away, and you can ask him to notice what happens to the image as his desire increases. Usually putting the person into a scenario that exaggerates the desire will make the driver more obvious. Some people give in to their compulsions so quickly that they don't have time to recognize what drives them.

One of the keys to helping someone access a compulsion so that you can get the information, is to access a compulsion-type state yourself. If you have a "ho-hum" attitude, and act cool and detached, as if you don't care about the object of their compulsion, your nonverbal behavior will tend to dissociate him from the experience and reduce his response. That will make it harder for your partner to get the compulsive response. If you communicate "compulsive state" through all your nonverbal behavior, he'll be more likely to get in there with you. "What do you need to do with that image to make you want it *more*, so that you're *drooling* over that luscious piece of chocolate?''

Often the driver will *result* in a "figure/ground" submodality difference. With Rachel, the chocolates got closer while the plate stayed in the same place. The chocolates also had a halo around them, which separated them from the background.

If the person doesn't find anything that compels him visually, check the other representational systems. Is there something auditory or kinesthetic? During the exercise, Charles was saying, "I don't get it. I don't notice anything different. I can't find how to change the way it pulls on me." I created some scenarios for him, like those I just described, but we couldn't find anything. I tested some of the standard submodalities: "Make it bigger, bring it closer," but none of those had any impact. Then I asked, "Well, do you *hear* anything?" and he was instantly aware of a voice. "Make it louder." "Oh, yeah, *that* does it!" So if the person doesn't notice any visual differences, ask him to check other representational systems.

Ruth: I have to have coffee, and I think it's all kinesthetic. Is that possible?

It's possible, but not very likely. Usually when people tell you "It's all kinesthetic," they're talking about the feeling of desire itself. We know *that's* a feeling. What we want to know is, "How does your brain create that feeling of desire? You probably don't get that feeling when you think about drinking motor oil. What's different?" Usually your image of the coffee itself is different.

If a kinesthetic feeling drove your compulsion to drink coffee, it would have to be a *tactile* or *proprioceptive* sensation—the feeling of coffee on your tongue, or in your mouth—that you need to identify, not the resulting meta-feeling of desire.

One smoker had a weird tactile sensation that started in his neck, climbed up, hit his head, and started covering him. The critical submodality was the *extent* of that sensation; as the sensation became more widespread, the compulsion to smoke got stronger. When I tried that, I didn't like it either! I might even smoke if I had that! (laughter) This tactile sensation was different than the feeling of desire. If you get a body sensation, test to be sure the sensation can be used to *create* the desire, and isn't just another description of the desire response itself.

What happened when you tried to simply decrease the driving submodality to eliminate the compulsion? Were any of you successful in doing that?

Man: I could decrease it for a while, but the feeling of compulsion always seemed to creep back.

That's what usually happens. If you're able to permanently eliminate it by simply decreasing the driving submodality, then it probably wasn't what we call a compulsion in the first place. It was probably something weaker, more like a desire. If any of you were successful in permanently eliminating a "compulsion" by just decreasing the driver, use some other compulsion to continue the exercise.

Most of you have identified exactly what drives your compulsions, and you have done this very thoroughly, which is appropriate when you're first learning the pattern. You need to take the time to explore it. After you've done this a few times, you will begin to be able to identify the driving submodality quickly by observing the client, and you won't have to test such a long list of submodalities.

When you ask about submodalities, keep your language precise. Ask for exactly what you want to know. It isn't specific enough to say, "Make it bigger. Now what do you think?" "Oh, now I really like it." That's not what you want to know. You want to know, "When you make it bigger, *do you have to have it more; are you more compelled?*" Be sure to ask precisely for the response you're interested in. You don't care if the change produces some other response. Ann *liked* the image of ice cream more when she made it bigger, but she didn't feel more like she had to eat it. Sometimes the person will change the picture and suddenly get sad, or feel some other emotion. This may be a more intense response, but *it isn't the one you need to know about.*

Compulsions

Compulsions usually have the following sequence of four elements:

1. *Representation* of the object of the compulsion. Usually this is visual, less often auditory or kinesthetic. This lets the person know it's time to have the compulsion.

2. *Submodality Distortion of the Representation.* The person alters his internal representation in a specific way. Although more than one submodality may be involved, and it may occur in any or all representational systems, usually there is a single analogue submodality, often visual, that drives the compulsion and makes it compelling.

3. *Feeling of Compulsion.* This is the kinesthetic meta-feeling of having to do something, and not having any choice about it.

4. *Compulsive Behavior.* The feeling of compulsion often leads to a behavior that the person *has to do*, like biting nails, eating chocolates, etc.

If you are dealing with a more general emotional response such as anger, it's possible that the person doesn't have any specific behavioral response.

Demonstration: Eliminating a Compulsion

Now let's go on to demonstrate the Compulsion Blowout. We'll use the information you gathered earlier in order to eliminate a compulsion. Who has a compulsion you'd like to get rid of?

Fred: I do.

Do you have the submodality drivers already identified? (Yes.) Come on up. Can we know the content?

Fred: Sure. I love pistachios. I can't even talk about them without drooling!

Good. What do you have to do to make yourself want them more? You're skilled at this already, right? (Fred sighs and his eyes look up.) You're seeing something, right? What are you doing to the image to make yourself want it more?

Fred: I was getting a sharper and sharper focus.

And that does it? It seems to! Did your partner test any other submodalities?

Woman: Yes. When we had him zoom in on one pistachio and make it very big, it made a difference.

All right. Three submodalities have been mentioned: focus, zooming in, and size. What I need to do is either find the one that makes all the others happen automatically, or find the one that's the most significant. Fred, what do you see to start with, a picture of a whole bunch of pistachios, or one, or what?

Fred: It's a plateful.

Okay, a plate full of pistachios. I'd like you to zoom in on one pistachio. . . . Yes, we can see from watching him that zooming in gets a strong response.

Now zoom back to normal, and then make the whole image bigger. Notice your response.

Fred (in a low, breathy voice): You mean, . . . see more of them?

That's not what I meant, but you could try it out. What happens when you do that? . . .

Fred: I'm surprised that didn't make much difference.

We're not getting the same nonverbal response, are we? He doesn't look as compelled. Now Fred, try taking the plate of pistachios and make every one of them bigger. . . . That also doesn't make him respond as much as zooming in. Now make the pistachios regular size, and make the plate of pistachios very clear. . . .

No, that doesn't do it either. Let's check another submodality. Take the plate of pistachios and move it closer, instead of zooming in.

Fred: I can even smell them when I do that!

But does it make you want them more? We aren't interested in whether you can smell them. . . .

Fred: No, I don't want them more.

Zooming in is what gets you, isn't it? Everyone's salivating! We should have done this before lunch.

Fred: I had a pistachio sandwich. (laughter)

Before we blow out your compulsion, I want you to know that you will still have the choice of eating and enjoying pistachios when you want to. You just won't be compelled. Given that, are you sure you want to eliminate your compulsion, or is it so much fun that you want to keep it forever?

Fred: No, no, no. I can't have any pistachios in the house, because I'll eat them all at one sitting. I'd like to be able to keep some around.

OK. Now, Fred, you've got an image of a plate of pistachios, right? Here's what I want you to do. Take the image of the plate, and zoom in all the way on one pistachio, very fast, to make yourself *really* want it. Then start over with seeing the entire plate of pistachios, and quickly zoom in again.

I want to warn you that as you do this, it will increase your feeing of compulsion. If at some time you feel like it's getting so intense that you can't stand it, that means that you're doing the right thing, and you only have a little more to do.

Zoom in over and over until you want that pistachio more than you've ever wanted one before. Repeat this until you notice a qualitative shift in your response. . . . Faster and faster. . . . That's right, even faster, until you can't do it any faster. . . . That's right. Great! Something shifted a little while ago already, right?

Fred: Too big. It gets too big and goes away. There's nothing to reach out for any more.

That's one way to put it. Now, let's talk a bit, and then test.

Fred: Why doesn't somebody get some pistachios? (laughter)

Good idea; we'll have a real test! When you think of pistachios now, do you want them? . . .

Fred: No. I can't zoom in. I just see the whole plate now. Usually I see the plate and then zoom in on one single pistachio and grab it. But now I just see the plate.

Are you sure? Try to get it back.

Fred: Maybe I can work on it. (laughter)

Sally: What if there were a plate of pistachios right up next to you? . . .

Fred: Something's different.

Sally: The location of the image has changed. It was different before he did the zooming.

Good observation. When he visualizes pistachios *now*, he looks in a different location than he did before. This is a further confirmation. The pistachios are now in the location where the non-compelling image was. Does anyone know where we can get some pistachios?

Fred: You can buy them down on the first floor of the hotel.

All right. We'll get some and try it later this afternoon! Does anyone have any questions for Fred?

Bill: Fred, what were your internal sensations as you did the blowout?

Fred: I'd see the plate and then I'd zoom in on one single extremely clear pistachio. And the more I did it, the more it felt like something holding me back.

And then what happened?

Fred: Well, it wasn't a comfortable feeling. That one pistachio got bigger and bigger, and somehow it got to the size where it didn't seem natural.

That is a typical description of going over threshold. Your brain has a threshold at both ends of the spectrum. Let's use the example of someone who is compelled to eat chocolate, and size is the driving submodality. If her picture of chocolate is *very* small, it just looks like a black speck, and it won't have any effect. Making the picture a little larger allows her to go over a lower threshold as her brain recognizes it as something to be compelled about. As she increases the size, she feels more and more compelled, until the chocolate looks *too* big, and her response will go over an upper threshold. When it's *too* big, her brain no longer recognizes it as something she's compelled to have. Now her brain looks at it and puts it in a different category, like "ridiculous" or "gross." If you do this rapidly enough, the shift becomes permanent.

When we first learned this method, Steve used it to blow out his compulsion to read the comics. He *had* to read every comic strip, even the ones he didn't like. If he tried to skip one he didn't particularly like, it was as if a gray moldy substance would grow around that comic. The farther he got from that comic, the bigger the mold grew, and the more Steve felt pulled back toward the comic. So he made the mold grow bigger and bigger, very rapidly, until it simply didn't compel him any more. Then he went back and tested; when he skipped the comic he didn't care about, it was as if there were a little black pile of decayed mold over the cartoon. His experience had changed permanently.

The Compulsion Blowout is an example of a threshold pattern, in which you take a very intense response and *increase* it, rather than try to reduce or eliminate it. You increase it so much and so rapidly that at a certain point it goes over threshold and it "pops." This is very much like someone blowing up a balloon. For a while, each breath you put in makes the balloon bigger. However, if you keep blowing air into the balloon, it will finally pop. Once it pops, you can't get the balloon back by taking out that last breath of air. In fact, you won't be able to get it back at all without a great deal of trouble! Another example of this is bending a piece of metal or wire back and forth until it breaks. Once it's broken, you can't get the piece of wire back by just unbending it.

There are two ways to do a blowout:

1. A single submodality increase.
2. The repeated ratchet method.

The first way is to rapidly increase the driving submodality to such an extreme that the kinesthetic response passes an upper threshold and pops— which is what Steve did. If Fred's driving submodality had been size, he could have taken that plate of pistachios and very rapidly made the picture bigger and bigger, until his response popped.

The ratchet method, which I used with Fred, is really doing the first method over and over, in rapid succession. With this method you take the driving submodality and increase it very rapidly. Then you start again with the picture in its original state and rapidly increase the submodality again. You do this over and over in rapid succession to amplify the kinesthetic response of being compelled. To give you an example, let's say increasing the brightness drives the compulsion. I start by having the person see the image, and then rapidly increase the brightness. Then I want the person to immediately see the image in its original brightness, and gradually make it brighter again. You do this over and over, very rapidly, until something pops. After the pop, his response changes and he is no longer compelled.

This works very much like using a jack on a car. You push the jack handle down, and the car goes up a little bit. You push the jack handle down again, and the car goes up a bit more. With each push of the jack handle, the car goes higher and higher. The jack handle is like the submodality that you are ratcheting: size, brightness, etc. The car going up corresponds to the increase in your kinesthetic feeling of being compelled.

In both methods, we're very rapidly increasing the response of wanting something until the person crosses a threshold and his response breaks. When the person's compulsion pops, you can usually see a shift from the outside, too. You can see his nonverbal response intensify and intensify, and then suddenly it stops increasing and starts to decrease.

With both methods you vary a submodality over a range to increase the kinesthetic response. That's why you need an analogue submodality rather than a digital one.

The inertia, or duration, in the kinesthetic system is what makes the ratchet method work. You can change internal images or sounds very rapidly, without the old one lingering around. However, if you get a really intense feeling, it takes much longer to shift to some other feeling. Lots of hormonal and chemical changes go along with intense emotional states, and it takes your body a little while to return to a neutral state. Let's say, for example, that you are convinced you are in grave danger, and your body starts producing adrenalin. If you then realize that there actually isn't any danger, it still takes you quite a while to calm down kinesthetically.

Since feelings tend to last, you have time to very quickly go back to a small picture and make it bigger again, over and over. Each time you increase the size of the picture, your feelings start where you left off before, and increase further.

Sam: So it will not work slowly?

Right. You will increase the intensity of the compulsion, and you may only make it worse!

Fred: If you had done it slowly, I'd think that would have made me want pistachios more, because every time we experimented with my submodalities, phew! I'd salivate, and I wanted to keep the picture coming.

People often make the mistake of going too slowly. If you do this too slowly, you could end up increasing a person's compulsion, and leaving him there: "Ohhh! Now I *really* want pistachios!"

Fred: You too, huh? (laughter)

So if the blowout isn't working, you're probably not having the person go fast enough. Now, how can you get someone to go faster?

Dennis: By talking faster and faster.

Right. If you talk veerryy sslloooowly, the person probably won't go over threshold. You can also indicate the speed with a rapid hand gesture or sound. You could snap your fingers, or say "Very fast—pffft!" or do anything else that lets him know that "fast" means *split-second*! "Fast" doesn't mean five seconds in contrast to five years. A nonverbal gesture can communicate the specific submodality change, as well as the speed.

If you want him to move the picture closer, you can put your hand where the picture will start, with your palm facing him, to represent his picture, and then move your hand rapidly toward him. You can say, "Let your picture move rapidly toward you, like this." If you want him to make the picture bigger, you can use both your hands to frame a small picture, and then rapidly move your hands outward, expanding the frame. You can then use these gestures and sounds as anchors to assist your partner in doing this quickly. It is also helpful to use hypnotic language patterns to imply that the process will begin to go faster and faster on its own.

You can act a bit ridiculous when you're demonstrating this process, because that will give your partner permission to act ridiculous, too. He may need to act a little weird in order to go over threshold.

Bill: How do you decide which blowout technique to use: single increase or the ratchet method?

Some submodalities can increase without limit. Size is one; you could theoretically keep increasing size and never have to stop. You can generally blow out this type of compulsion by simply increasing the relevant submodality until the response pops.

However, other submodalities have a limit to how much you can change them in a particular direction. You can only zoom in so much, for example. With a submodality like that, you're much more likely to need the ratchet method. You can always try a single increase, and then wait a little while and test. If the compulsion isn't already broken, you can go on to use the ratchet method.

Make sure you ratchet in *one direction only*. One woman was compelled to read the New York Times, and she didn't want to. Hearing an internal voice get softer increased her desire to read the newspaper, and she couldn't get the response to pop. She was attempting to ratchet by softening the voice, then making it gradually get louder, then gradually softer, etc. If you do this, you will make the desire response get stronger, then weaker, then stronger. I knew she was doing this by watching her hand gestures, which went back and forth gradually, when she described trying to blow out her response. Usually you can tell by someone's nonverbal gestures if they are going both ways with the submodality instead of one way only. What worked for her was making the voice softer, then hearing it begin loud and getting gradually softer. Then hearing it begin loud, and getting gradually softer, etc.

Dennis: Couldn't you get the compulsion back by just running the film of doing the blowout backwards?

Running the movie backwards won't work to undo this pattern. If you pop someone's response with this method, you can't simply go back the other way. Before you break someone's response, be absolutely sure he *wants* to have it broken. Explore what his life will be like without the compulsion, because once he's gone over threshold, he won't be able to get it back simply by going the other way. It's a little bit like dragging a large Christmas tree through a narrow door. If you decide you want to have the tree back where it was, you can't just push it back through the door. It's not that simple. We'll teach you how to build compulsions next, after you know how to break them.

Testing

After doing the blowout, be sure to wait a minute or two before testing. Sometimes the person doesn't notice right away that she has changed, because those feelings of compulsion will take a while to dissipate. When you ask her, "Are you still compelled?" she may answer, "I think I still am." Because the kinesthetic system has so much inertia, she may not immediately notice when she has gone over threshold.

If you test immediately, you don't necessarily have a good test. It depends on how intense the kinesthetic feelings have to get before reaching threshold. If the feeling of compulsion is gone immediately, then you can be confident you blew out the compulsion. But if the feeling is still there, you may need to wait a little while and test again.

If you wait a couple of minutes, the kinesthetic system has enough time to settle down again, and she can notice that she can no longer generate the feeling of compulsion. The connection between the image and the kinesthetic reaction is severed. It's broken, different.

Go ahead with the exercise. Let us know if you have any difficulties and would like assistance.

Exercise Outline:

1. Be sure you have identified the driving submodality.
2. Use either the single increase or the ratchet method on the driving submodality until it goes over threshold.
3. Pause and test.

Discussion

There are many aspects to using this pattern ecologically and effectively, so let's talk a while.

Sam: In our group it was like working really hard toward an orgasm, and it would never come.

So to speak. Was the compulsion different later when you tested?

Sam: Yeah. It was gone. But there wasn't any tremendous break-through or anything like that.

I like that description. Many people don't notice when they go over threshold, particularly when the response has to get very intense before it pops. But if you wait a while, so your kinesthetic system has enough time to settle down again, you can notice that you are no longer compelled.

Tempo

Woman: Is it possible to do this too fast?

Usually people do this process too *slowly*, and you need to speed them up. Once in a while, though, someone actually does this pattern too fast. If someone is doing it very fast and it's not working, he may need to slow down enough to generate a robust kinesthetic response. I've used this method many times, and I've only needed to slow someone down twice. They seemed to be changing the submodalities so rapidly that they didn't have time for a full kinesthetic response.

Bob: My compulsion was increasing so fast that I wondered if I was doing the right thing, and if it would *ever* pop. Finally I couldn't control the speed at which it was going. There was a ringing in my ears, and it actually went "Boom!"

Remember this when working with someone else. When the feeling starts getting really intense, if she becomes unnerved and tries to make the feeling less intense, it's not going to work. Your setup needs to include a warning of what to expect, so that she knows she's doing the right thing when the feeling of compulsion increases, and she doesn't back off. When I use this method with clients, I usually explain the method first by using the balloon-popping and wire-bending analogies. This prepares the person to continue to increase the feeling until it pops. We wanted to demonstrate to you that the method also works with little advance explanation, and we were watching for any sign that Fred was backing off.

Be sure that you don't leave someone in a state of *increased* compulsion. If you have the person pump up her response, but not enough to pop it, you can actually increase her compulsion. Usually this means that you didn't go fast enough.

Sometimes each individual ratchet doesn't go quite far enough, or the person stops just short of blowing his response. Once someone told me, "I've been making the picture as big as the known universe, and it's still not working." "As big as the *known* universe" implies some kind of stopping point, so I told him, "Do it again, and this time let the picture continue to get *bigger* than the known universe." He did that once, and his response was broken.

Sarah: What gets "broken" when you do this? What "pops"?

You're breaking the connection between the person's picture— or sound or feeling—and his kinesthetic response. He'll still be able to make an image, but it won't pull on him in the same way.

Strong Emotional Responses

We asked you to do this with a minor compulsion for learning purposes, but this method is equally effective with major compulsions. It also works with strong emotional responses. People have used this pattern to eliminate compulsions involving bingeing, cigarettes, being too attached to someone, anger, etc. It's excellent for responses that are so intense that you can't get them to just decrease, which is how people usually try to deal with them.

Although this method works well for things like intense anger, be careful if you use it for that. With some people there is some risk of violence if you increase their anger. Many people would not become violent, no matter how angry they got, so they wouldn't be dangerous to you, but it's something to be cautious about. Providing the person with a good setup can help avoid violence: prepare the person to do the blowout so fast that he will go over threshold before he has time to smash anything. If he goes too slowly and gets stuck in a hyped-up state, he could become violent. If you have any doubts, you might want to have someone really strong around who can rescue you, just in case.

One of our students has used this pattern with suicidal and homicidal compulsions, and he says it's never permanently made a compulsion stronger. However, because of the possible danger of leaving the person in a state of increased compulsion, I'd be *very careful*. Unless you're very experienced both with this method and with suicidal or violent people, we *strongly* recommend referring these people to someone else who has the necessary background.

Unpleasant Responses

When you use this method with pleasurable responses—desire for food, sex, smoking, etc.—you usually have no trouble getting the person to intensify his response. When you use this with responses that the person doesn't like, it can be more difficult, because people don't usually want to experience something like intense anger. In this situation, your advance framing is much more important. They won't want to do it unless they know that the reason you want them to feel intense anger *now*, is so that they'll never need to feel uncontrollably angry again. They will still have the choice of getting angry, but won't be driven uncontrollably by their own anger. The justification for them to experience a few seconds of anger now is so they can avoid being overwhelmed by anger many times in the future.

This threshold effect has already been utilized under the name "implosion therapy." However, implosion therapists don't know about submodalities. They try to overcome phobias by using *content*, instead of increasing a driver submodality. They create scenarios in which rats climb up the client's arm and into her mouth, etc. If you use content instead of submodalities, the process is much clumsier. You can't go as rapidly, you can't go to the submodality extremes as well, and as far as I know, the people doing implosion therapy don't know about the ratchet method and the need for speed. Because of this it's more likely that clients will get stuck in an intensified state, and not go *over* threshold. Implosion therapist's theory of how it works is also different. They believe they are extinguishing a response by providing the stimulus without the real-world consequences. If that were true, phobias would extinguish automatically!

Ecology

Let's talk about ecology. Where are the ecology considerations in this pattern?

Al: As an example from today's exercise, a woman in my group was compelled to eat salty things at night. Her husband likes to play Pac-Man in the evenings, and he wants her to stay up with him. She was sitting there in the chair falling asleep with nothing to do.

·So the eating might give her something to do, so that she could stay awake and spend time with her husband.

Al: Right.

What would happen if you blow out that compulsion and now she just falls asleep?

Al: Well, her husband might be angry that she doesn't stay up with him.

Right, and their relationship could deteriorate. There's actually *nothing* in the compulsion blowout pattern that takes care of ecology. It's one of the few NLP patterns that eliminates a response without putting anything in its place. What could you do to take care of ecology in this situation?

Al: How about using the swish pattern?

Exactly. This is a great time to use a swish to send her brain in a more useful direction.

Al: What would you use as a cue image if you've blown out the compulsion image?

Use the image that originally created the compulsion, and the same driving submodality, even though this image won't elicit the compulsive response anymore. If size compelled the person before, run a swish pattern using size. Whenever you have any indication that the compulsion does something positive for the person—such as this woman's compulsion to eat helping her stay up with her husband—it's imperative to do a swish after the compulsion blowout. Have her see the her that has lots of other choices for enhancing her relationship with her husband. Even when you don't know that a compulsion has a positive function, it's a good idea to do a swish just to be safe. It doesn't take long to do, and it could be very important. We routinely use the swish pattern after doing a compulsion blowout.

Sarah: Why not just use the swish? Why do you need to bother with a compulsion blowout, too?

Sometimes a response is so strong that it's very hard to get the swish pattern or another method to work. With a very intense response, you sometimes need to do a compulsion blowout first. This breaks up the old pattern, and gives the swish a chance to work. This is what Richard Bandler did in his client session videotape titled "Anticipatory Loss." (See Appendix II) When he used the swish alone, it didn't work. Then he had the client "white out" the picture that caused the problem and followed that by repeating the swish pattern. That time it worked.

When we first learned the swish, Steve spent about ten minutes doing the standard swish with our typesetter, who was smoking about a pack and a half a day. After that, she cut back to about one cigarette a day. Over a period of months, she found her smoking gradually creeping up to two or three cigarettes per day. This was about the time we learned the compulsion blowout. Connirae was taking some typesetting in, and she spent about twenty minutes with the typesetter identifying driver submodalities, and blowing them out. While auditory submodalities seemed strongest in this case, she blew out some visual ones as well, just to be sure. In testing immediately, neither Connirae nor the typesetter could tell for sure if her response was different. However, later, she tried smoking, and said she "couldn't finish a cigarette "

Man: A man in my group hesitated to blow out his compulsion until he decided on something that he could replace it with.

Good idea! When someone hesitates about blowing something out, or he doesn't get into it quickly and easily, be alert. It could mean there are ecology concerns. Explore a bit—is there any useful purpose to the compulsive behavior? If so, make sure that he understands that he will end up with other behaviors which serve the same purpose. You might even help him develop these new choices before you do the compulsion blowout.

Generalization

Woman: We were afraid to blow out my partner's compulsion, because I was concerned that it might blow out all of her motivation, not just the compulsion. Wouldn't it have been a bad thing to blow that out?

This is a question about generalization. It depends upon how the client is thinking about her experience. In another seminar we asked everyone to pick something trivial to blow out, and one man picked "cleaning." He didn't want to be such a compulsive cleaner. However, when he talked about it he called it blowing out his "*orderliness.*" When you hear that kind of thing—if your partner says something about *motivation*, or uses some other broad nominalization that could go across a wide range of contexts like a criterion, be *extremely* cautious about using this pattern. *Orderliness* is so broad that any change is likely to generalize all over the place, which can create problems. It certainly did for him!

He came back the next day and said, "Yesterday I blew out orderliness. It was just a simple thing, but then I found that I didn't drive home very well." Another participant said, "Yes, I drove behind him, and I can verify what he is saying!" For him, orderliness was also a quality of driving; his driving was also "orderly." If you ask someone what his compulsion is and he gives you a big nominalization, your ecology buzzers should go off. Make sure that he's blowing out *only* what he wants to blow out. If you have any doubts, talk to him about contextualizing it. "In what situations do you still want to be orderly?" "Well, when I'm driving my car." "Oh. OK, so it's *only* when you clean dishes that you want to be less orderly; you *only* want to blow out your compulsion to do the *dishes*, is that right?" "Well, I also clean up the bathroom too often; I don't want to have to do that either." This gets him to visualize two categories: one where he wants to eliminate his compulsion, and the other where he wants to keep it. As long as he has these two contexts cleanly sorted, he can blow out *only* the ones where he wants his compulsion eliminated.

The compulsion blowout is a technique you want to use in a very circumscribed way. Since this method doesn't install what else to do instead, you don't usually want it to generalize everywhere in the person's life.

Bill: So are you saying the compulsion blowout isn't generative?

Not in the sense that the swish is. It just breaks a compulsion. It can be extremely important and useful, and it can allow you to do all kinds of other things. But this pattern is not generative; you don't want it to be.

Bill: What happened to the orderliness guy?

We had him re-install the orderliness compulsion in the context of driving. We're going to teach you how to *create* compulsions next, but we want to be very sure you know how to break them first, so that you can get rid of one if you make a mistake and create the wrong one. We urge you to be very cautious in using these patterns until you have already learned many other basic supporting NLP techniques.

Auditory or Kinesthetic Drivers

Some of you noticed that even though your partner blew out a compulsion visually, they could still get it back. Sometimes they're getting it back via another representational system. When we were first learning about compulsions, one woman blew out her compulsion visually, and although she couldn't get it back visually, she could get it back auditorily, with a voice. When she blew it out auditorily, she found that she could still get it back using kinesthetic tempo. Once she blew that out, however, it was gone. She blew out another compulsion using only kinesthetic tempo, and found she couldn't get the compulsion back either visually or auditorily. Blowing it out kinesthetically also blew it out in the other systems. This indicates that for her the principal driver was in the kinesthetic system.

You can approach this in two different ways. You can test very thoroughly in all representational systems for the most powerful driving submodality that produces the compulsion. Or, you can use a visual submodality that you know produces the compulsion, blow that out, and then check. Can the person get the compulsion back any other way? If he can get it back with a sound, blow that out. If he can still get it back with a feeling, blow that out. At least you'll know what representational system to use first the next time!

One seminar participant was able to recreate her compulsion by swishing herself back to the compelled state. We took care of that by swishing her somewhere else.

Woman: Can you give an example of blowing out feelings?

If kinesthetic tempo, such as tapping my foot, creates a compulsion, and the faster I tap the more compelled I feel, I could tap my foot faster and faster and faster—either actually on the outside, or in imagination on the inside—until the compulsion is blown out. If *extent* of a tactile feeling is what drives the compulsion response, I might feel only a pinpoint of the tactile feeling, and then have it spread out over my whole body until the compulsion pops.

One woman was revolted by her husband's touch. The closer the touch got to a particular "private" location on her body, the more revolted she felt. If you were to blow that out, you would have her start feeling the touch far away from that location, and quickly move the touch in closer, using the rachet method.

Be sure to check for ecology with something like that, though. I asked this woman, "Are you sure you want to have this blown out? Maybe your husband touches you in a very rough, insensitive way, and you need to be aware of it." At the time, she said, "No, he touches fine. I'm sure I don't want to have the revulsion." So I helped her eliminate the revulsion. Later on she told me it had worked for a while, and then her revulsion came back, and she realized that it *did* contain an important message about their relationship.

This is the stage at which many people think they've failed with a client. We think of this as the beginning of success. This woman, and you, now have important information about secondary gain that needs to be handled before any intervention will work permanently. This information hadn't been available to the woman before, but living for a short period of time without the revulsion brought it to her attention. Posing the ecology question alerted her to the possibility of a problem, future-pacing her to notice it if it occurred. Now you're in a position to design something that really works, and is fully ecological. We presented an example of doing this at the end of the swish chapter (Mary).

Out of Consciousness

One person I worked with couldn't get any conscious representation of what was compelling him. I had him pretend *as if* something was increasing his compulsion. I first gave him several examples of other people going over thresholds, so he was all set up. That kind of preparation is very important. I then had him *pretend* as if he was increasing the driving submodality in his own experience, and to increase it faster and faster until it popped. That worked for him.

Polarities

Remember when you learned how to deal with polarities in your Practitioner Training? For example, a bulimic typically has one part that wants to gorge, and another part that wants to starve and be thin. What do you think would happen if you used the compulsion blowout on only one of the two parts?

Sarah: The other part would probably take over.

Yes. If you blow out her attraction for food, and there is another part that wants to starve her, you could end up with an anorexic. Bulimia and anorexia are closely related, and often someone switches from one to the other "spontaneously." If someone has both an attraction and a repulsion for something, you need to be careful to blow out the *repulsion* as well. One way to test for two parts is to check for a *neutral* response after you've blown out the attraction. If you blow out attraction to potato chips, and then the person feels disgusted with potato chips, you're not done; you've got another part to deal with. If the person has a neutral response after you've blown that out—they look and act like they have choice—then you're done.

The other way to check is by all the usual signs of incongruence or multiple parts described in *Reframing*.

Making Something Important

A compulsion for something certainly organizes your behavior. Like other kinds of motivation, it directs and focuses your attention and efforts toward obtaining it. At the same time, a strong compulsion severely restricts your choices and is likely to create "tunnel vision."

Motivation toward an *outcome* provides you with much more flexibility in the specific way you satisfy it. In contrast, a compulsion is for a specific thing that you *hope* will satisfy your outcome(s). When you achieve the object of your desire, you often find that it doesn't provide all the benefits you expected. If you have to have a particular thing, you may pass up many other things that would be even more satisfying to you. Your efforts to get what you are compelled to have may even make the people around you miserable and drive them away. Many people who have been bitten by the "gold bug" have found this out the hard way. You can probably think of some time in your past when a compulsion of yours had unpleasant consequences.

Good salespeople are often very skilled at creating compulsions. One of the outcomes of the next exercise is to train you to be able to blow out your own responses, when you want to, on the spot. That will give you even more ability to run your own brain, free of undue influence from others. You can use the next exercise to find out how you make something important. After doing that, you will blow out the compulsion you just created. This exercise is usually done in pairs or trios, so that people can assist each other, but you can also do it by yourself.

Exercise

1. Important thing. Think of something that didn't matter to you once, but now is very important to you. For this exercise think of some *thing* (in contrast to an activity) that you "have to have." Find something that you almost drool over. You might very much want, or have to have, a certain painting, or piece of jewelry. A computer, a dress, a memento, or a car may be particularly important to you.

2. Unimportant thing. Think of something that isn't important to you. Be sure to choose something that is *neutral*, not something that is repulsive—important to you in a negative way. If you find an object aversive, it would be necessary to blow out your aversive response first to make it neutral. Pick something trivial that is nearby, such as a styrofoam cup, a pencil, or a magazine.

3. Contrastive analysis. Find the submodality differences between 1 and 2 above, and test to find out which of them are the most powerful in making the unimportant thing important. If you do this with someone else, be sure to calibrate to your partner's nonverbal shifts when he is talking about what is important to him, in contrast to when he is describing what is unimportant.

4. Creating a compulsion. Find out what has to be done to give this trivial and unimportnat thing a *lasting* importance. Make one submodality change at a time and then pause to test whether the change is temporary or lasting. Find out what it takes to make this thing important in a way that is *durable*.

5. Testing. Test whether you've gotten it there by imagining that someone else won't let you have it, or that someone else owns it and might sell it to you if you pay enough imagining that someone else won't let you have it, or that someone else owns it and might sell it to you if you pay enough for it.

6. Compulsion blowout. Now "blow out" the importance of this thing in one of two ways: either use the same submodalities you just used to make the neutral thing important, or if that doesn't work, use the same submodalities you used in the exercise on breaking compulsions.

If you want to gain more familiarity with how something becomes important to you, and more skill at blowing out your compulsions quickly, recycle through the last two steps of the exercise several times. This is a way to create "bullet-proof" sales resistance.

When something becomes durably important, it's because certain powerful submodalities have reached a lower threshold. Once this lower threshold has been reached, you can't make it unimportant by simply reducing the submodalities you increased. The compulsion blowout increases those same submodalities past a higher, second threshold in order to reach neutrality again.

Once you know which submodalities create a compulsion for someone, you can practice creating a compulsion conversationally—something that good salespeople do, usually unconsciously. When we first learned this pattern from Richard Bandler three years ago, he demonstrated with a man we'll call Ted. The submodalities that created a compulsion for Ted were brightness, and height in his visual field. If Ted heard a voice (internal or external) describe something in a Texas drawl, that would make his representation higher and brighter. Richard started describing an ordinary yellow chair that was at the seminar in a slow Texas drawl: "Ted, I'd like you to consider owning that yellow chair. I think it would be a *bright* idea to have that chair *up* in your office. It's *highly* interesting to *reflect* on how having that chair would let your clients *see* how you're coming *up* in the world. I wonder how the lights in your office would shine off that chair? What *rises* in your mind when you think of a yellow chair?"

As Richard was talking, he used congruent hand gestures and head movements that amplified the impact of the words. For instance, on the word "up" he would raise one hand about six inches and roll his head slightly up and back. Soon that ordinary yellow chair became *very* important to Ted. Ted can develop a compulsion for nearly *anything* that he sees higher and brighter in his mind. For someone else it may be anything that has a certain colored halo around it.

Some people have much more sales resistance because of the *structure* of how they create compulsions. For instance, Lara's method is to see the object under consideration in the center of several other images that indicate how she would actually make use of the object. Since she doesn't see the object out of context, it's much more difficult to get her to arbitrarily think of something as important. You have to build a lot of valid functional connections between the object and other outcomes in her life, and this will have to be done in ways that actually meet her criteria. A person like Lara will feel a need for relatively few things, and they will usually satisfy her criteria. Someone with a simpler structure for building a compulsion is more likely to feel a need for a lot of things, many of which will not actually satisfy his criteria, and they will end up unused in his closet or garage.

Usually your representation of an object changes to your "important" submodalities when you think that object meets your criteria for "important." When you see that it's useful enough, for example, it may pop out from the background. When it's enough fun, it rises, or when it's prestigious enough, it gets a halo around it. By directly asking someone to see the object as brighter, higher, or whatever, you are bypassing the person's criteria and going straight for the submodality coding that lets him know something matches his criteria.

Since you are bypassing the person's criteria, when you build a lasting compulsion in this way you need to be especially careful about ecology. Like the compulsion blowout, there is nothing in building compulsions that takes care of ecology. Although ecology is not taught in most sales trainings, whenever we teach sales we point out that the most important product you can sell is *satisfaction*. Satisfaction results in repeat business and referrals. With hype and high-pressure techniques you can sell ice-boxes to Eskimos—for a while. But when someone leaves you satisfied, he will tell his friends, because it's such a rare experience—whether or not you sell him anything.

We have included this section on building compulsions for several reasons. First, because it's interesting in itself. Second, it helps you understand more about how submodalities work in compulsions. Third, there may be a *few* times when you actually want to build a compulsion for someone; you'll know what to do if you blow out the wrong compulsion.

However, in most cases some other NLP intervention will be far more generative and useful for the person than building a blind compulsion for a specific thing. Specific compulsions usually restrict choice, making you into something of a robot. In contrast, most NLP interventions *add* choices and flexibility to your behavior, making you more human.

VI

"The Last Straw" Threshold Pattern

Do you know about that one straw that broke the camel's back? There are many other phrases that describe this kind of threshold. "That's one time too many," "You pushed me too far," "You went over the line this time!" "That tears it," "I've had it up to here!" When people go over this kind of threshold, it's as if they say, "Never again" to something. For example, when a woman decides to get a divorce, she has usually had a history of problems with her husband; she can ignore one screw-up, maybe two, three, four, or whatever. But eventually enough incidents stack up—like the straws on the camel's back—and finally she goes, "That's it. It's all over. I'm getting a divorce."

The same thing can happen with habits like smoking, drinking, and overeating. Someone wakes up every morning with a hacking cough, or has problems with other people. Then one morning finally he says, "Never again will I smoke." The overeater might feel unpleasantly stuffed, or rip the seams out of her clothes one time too many, and finally decide "Never again will I treat myself that way."

A woman in one of our seminars went out with a man who slapped her on their first date. She immediately constructed future pictures of him slapping her harder and more often if she kept dating him, so she ended that relationship right then and there. She got to "Never again!" from a single example. We call this "the *only* straw pattern." In this case, she needed only a single experience in the real world to push her over threshold; her brain did the rest. Other people add up many experiences until they reach some "magic number," and then they go over threshold. In contrast, some people never go over threshold, at least in some contexts.

115

If you know the structure of what a person does internally to go, "Never again," you can run different content through the same pattern to get a behavioral change. Some people have trouble going over threshold when they should; knowing how to do it allows them do it voluntarily. Getting rid of unwanted habits is an obvious application of this pattern, but it has other uses, too. For example, people stick with jobs they can't stand, when it might actually be more useful for them to go over threshold, quit, and get into a job they enjoy.

People in abusive relationships often know that they should get out, but don't take any steps to do it. They get abused over and over and over. They're essentially trapped because they never say, "Never again." Understanding how they go over threshold with something else can allow you to help them go over threshold with abuse, so they can congruently say, "That's it; I'm not taking any more."

In the compulsion blowout you take the feeling of wanting a cigarette, or the desire for chocolates, and intensify it until it goes past the point where the brain recognizes it as motivation to smoke or eat. You *intensify the desire or need* to do a behavior until your response pops.

The last straw pattern is also a threshold pattern, but what you use to build to a threshold is reversed. Rather than amplifying the desire to do a behavior, you amplify wanting *not* to do it until you reach a threshold. Usually this is done by accumulating representations of the unpleasantness of continuing to do the behavior.

To give you a specific example of how this works, we're going to demonstrate how to elicit someone's threshold pattern.

Demonstration of Eliciting Crossing Threshold

OK, do we have somebody who went "Never again" in the past, and would like to find out how you did it? We'll want some content for this, so pick something that you're comfortable sharing. We don't need a lot of content; just enough to get the idea.

(The following transcript is edited from a videotape of an Advanced Submodalities Training in October, 1986. This segment, as well as additional discussion, is also available as an unedited videotape: See Appendix I. Bobbi had lived with a man for four years, when she finally went, "Never again." After that she never spoke to him again.)

Connirae: Did you also consider leaving this man a number of times? (*Bobbi:*   Yes, yes.) And did you get to the point where you thought you were going to leave, but then you stayed?

Bobbi: Yes, I even left him a couple of times, but then he weaseled his way back in—I allowed him to weasel his way back in.

Connirae: Perfect. So we want you to think of one time when you thought, "Never again," but then he weaseled his way back, and also think of the time when "This was really it." We're going to gather information from Bobbi about what was necessary for her to do in her mind, in order to get to the point of reaching threshold and crossing it. Notice that this often happens over a long period of time. This makes eliciting it a little bit tricky. You don't need to know everything a person did from start to finish.

Steve: This is a bit like eliciting someone's strategy for procrastination: if you get every detail, it takes you a very, very long time!

Connirae: It could take you years!

Steve: Because reaching and crossing threshold typically takes place over a period of time, we're deliberately dividing the process into three stages. One is reaching threshold, where she thinks, "Oh, I'm not going to see that guy again," but she does. The second stage is crossing threshold— the process that gets her to cross over the line and say, "That's it! I've had it! No more!" The third stage is discovering what to do next. What new behavior is possible now that the threshold has been crossed?

Connirae: So, Bobbi, I'd like you to go back to the time when you were still in love. Let's put a frame around this experience; that you're going to get out of it again, right? Go back to when you were still in love, and this is what you wanted, and very quickly let your experience go through reaching and crossing threshold, just for your own information. Notice what happens. . . .

(Bobbi closes her eyes and sits for a few moments.)

Connirae: What do you notice that you do, as you go through that, in order to reach threshold?

Bobbi: I go back and forth. (She nods her head left and right.)

Connirae: Between what?

Bobbi: Between what he says (nodding slightly to her left) and what he does (nodding to her right and opening her eyes). Between what he says (hand gesturing left), and what he does (hand gesturing right).

Connirae: So you heard some words—

Bobbi: His words were nice (hand gesturing straight ahead); his actions were crappy (hand gesturing far right).

Connirae: OK, when you hear the words, do you also have a representation of what they mean?

Bobbi (closing eyes briefly): Let me see. . . . Yes, certainly, to myself.

Connirae: She's gesturing back and forth as if it's in the same representational system. She's mentioning words, but she looks like she's pointing to pictures. My guess is that she has pictures of what these words mean.

Bobbi: Uh-huh, words and pictures, both.

Connirae: So she actually has two sets of pictures that she's comparing: the internal pictures that she makes of what her boyfriend is saying, and the pictures of what he actually does. So it looks like you go back and forth, comparing these representations sequentially.

Bobbi: Yes. It's like he'd say one thing (her right hand gestures straight ahead), but then his actions didn't match what he'd said, or they'd change (her hand sweeps to the right). We'd have another talk, and he'd say something else, and then his actions would be different. (Her hand gestures straight ahead again, and then sweeps right, but at a higher level.) It would go on like that (repeating the hand gesture at a still higher level) until finally, *Uhh*!

Connirae: Notice that this time her gestures are higher in space. Do you see that?

Steve: What triggers this change? When he does something good or says something you like, or when he does something that you didn't like?

Bobbi: When he does something that I don't like; he does something (holding up right hand) that doesn't match the picture of his words (holding up left hand). Whenever he did that, and it didn't match at all, we'd have another argument. He would say he was sorry and he'd never do that again, and he'd make promises (right hand gesturing left) but then he wouldn't keep them (hand sweeping to the right). And I'd look at those (she looks and gestures to her right), and I'd go, "Well, he's not doing that (gesturing right) even though he says this," (looking and gesturing to left with left hand) and that would make me angrier.

Connirae: And then?

Bobbi: I'd go up a level (raising head and both hands slightly). The argument would get more intense the next time.

Steve: When you say you go "up a level," does it actually rise in your visual field?

Bobbi: Oh yeah (gesturing up with right hand).

Connirae: Do you see the other incidents at the same time, or only the top one, or what?

Bobbi: I see them all. They build up on top of each other.

Connirae: So each time he does it, the next time you can see that one, but there's another one on top of it.

Bobbi: Right, it's a continuum, building.

Steve: When you make that sweeping gesture from left to right, what's in it? Is there a picture, another picture, and then something else? Or are there just two distinct pictures?

Bobbi (sweeping her right hand to the right): There are pictures of multiple actions. Whenever we would have an argument, we would talk afterwards and we would basically reset a new frame (gesturing with both hands to her left), a frame that he and I would work within, with each other, right? We'd come to an agreement and that would be nice—we'd have a plan and a frame. And then it would start. There would be this one action (gesturing slightly to the right of the frame) that wouldn't fit in this frame. There would be one mismatch, and then another, and another (gesturing a bit farther to the right for each mismatch).

Connirae: Good. So there are multiple pictures of mismatches over here (gesturing to Bobbi's right). This is a threshold within a threshold pattern. You have a positive frame, and then how many pictures of mismatches does it take before you go, "That's too many. We're going up a level?"

Bobbi: A lot. Less as I get older, but it used to be a lot.

Connirae: How did you know it was time for a confrontation? Did there have to be a certain number of pictures, or did they change in quality to let you know, "Now we've got to confront each other and set a new frame?"

Bobbi: I would get a feeling of being "locked in."

Steve: But what gave you that feeling?

Bobbi (moving head left and right): I think looking back and forth like this. Seeing him promise things (gesturing left) and then break his word (gesturing right). It was like breaking (both hands gesture repeatedly as if breaking a stick) his word each time. It would get so bad—there would be so many breaks that it would—Oh! that it would shatter the picture (gesturing to the left-hand "plan" picture). And then we went up to the next level.

Connirae: Good. Usually you'll find this kind of digital change, some kind of a qualitative difference, at the point that the person goes over a threshold. So Bobbi adds her mismatch pictures one at a time, and then the whole frame shatters, and she goes up a level.

Steve: At that point, you'd have another confrontation and make a new plan. And then you'd go through the whole sequence again at the new level, right?

Bobbi: That's right. It looks awful.

Connirae: How do you know that it's time to go "Never again" to the whole relationship? Is it a matter of how many of these levels stack up?

Bobbi: I don't know. I never looked into it before. . . . Let me see (She closes her eyes briefly, and her head moves left and right, repeatedly). He just got "that look" that someone gets when he's apologetic, and I just said—(both hands gesture in a large scissors motion.) We didn't even get into a conversation.

Steve: Now picture his look. (*Bobbi:*   Mmhmm.) What did you do inside that got you to the point where you didn't even talk to him?

Bobbi: OK, wait a second. . . . I saw all the breaks (hand sweeping up).

Connirae: All the breaks simultaneously?

Bobbi: Umhmm. And all this. (Her hand sweeps to the right.)

Connirae: And then what happened?

Bobbi: In each of the broken pictures, I saw his face. He was saying, "And I'm going to work this out," and apologizing.

Connirae: Now how is this different from the time when you had the confrontation and you moved out but you came back again?

Bobbi: I never looked at all the pictures at once.

Connirae: What did you look at those times?

Bobbi: Well, I looked at each one, and only the one before it in the stack. I had the others stored, but I didn't look at them. I didn't really look and go, "Oh, crap!" I would only look at the last one and go, "Well . . ." I was always really flexible, wanting to work things out, and I wouldn't want to look at the whole thing even though I knew it was there. And then there was one point when he made that apologetic face, and I saw *all* those things that he did, and I went, "*Uhh!*"

Steve: What happened right *after* that? Here's where she gets to the crossing.

Bobbi: There was a snap, and I disconnected from him.

Steve: How did you disconnect?

Bobbi: The way I connect to everyone is with a light fiber that's like a cord (gesturing out from her navel)—which is the way I connect to everything that I'm attached to.

Connirae: So that cord broke?

Bobbi: *Totally* in his case. Almost always I keep a strand left, that's dark, that holds the picture there just in case things might get nice again.

Steve: Now when the cord breaks, does something change in your visual representation?

Bobbi: Absolutely.

Steve: Does it fly off into infinity, or does it go blank . . .

Connirae: Or shatter, or white out . . . ?

Bobbi: It loses all its light. The picture is lit from my cord, and when I break the cord, the picture goes dark and it's no longer there. It doesn't live for me in my mind any more.

Connirae: OK, the cord is gone and the picture has blacked out. How do you know what's next?

Bobbi: I remember saying, "I don't ever want to do that again with anyone." . . . And then my next words to myself were— because I remember it really clearly—"I'm worth a lot more than that, so I'm going to go and work on myself."

Connirae: What's your representation of that?

Bobbi: I look different in it (looking ahead and slightly up).

Steve: Can you describe this a little bit? So you saw yourself?

Bobbi: Mmhmm. I saw myself looking more resourceful, more successful (gesturing with both hands in front of her at chest level).

Connirae (to audience): Does this sound familiar?

Steve: What has she done?

Various people in the audience: A swish!

Connirae: Yes. In comes the picture of who she will be.

Bobbi: And then the picture becomes very light and sparkly—my favorite submodalities.

Connirae: Exactly! She sees a picture of herself with access to more resources, as a person who can successfully manage relationships. This picture serves to move her in a new direction.

Bobbi: As soon as I got that image real clearly, then there are the steps to get there (gesturing to a series of pictures from her to the self-image picture)—which is the way I motivate myself. Then all the little pictures came down—the steps of what I needed to do to get there—and they all got real bright.

Steve: And from then on, it's a piece of cake. Wonderful. I've never seen this one before. Thanks a lot, Bobbi.

Connirae: This is an interesting threshold pattern, because it's a nested one.

Steve: There's one threshold here, when the ideal picture shatters and she confronts him and they build a new plan. Then there is the second threshold where she sees all these reruns, and the whole thing gets dark.

Exercise

Now we want you all to do what we did with Bobbi: find out how *you* use submodalities to cross threshold irreversibly. With Bobbi we used one content area, a relationship, to find out how she *reached* threshold. We used the same content area to learn about the later stage; the process of *crossing* threshold and moving toward a representation of a new alternative.

Another way to get the same information is to use different content areas for each of these two stages. You could think of one situation where you *reached* a threshold. You decide to quit smoking but somehow you keep finding yourself smoking. Then you could think of a different situation in which you actually *crossed* threshold permanently. Your car broke down once too many times, so you bought a new one, or someone you trusted cheated you, so you never trusted him again.

Put yourself into the past situation to discover which submodalities changed as you went through the process of reaching and crossing threshold, and how you represented the new alternative. Your goal is to learn the submodality *structure* of this process in sufficient detail that you could run *any* content through it.

After you have elicited your partner's threshold pattern, we want you to test whether you have it all by running some new content through it. Take a situation where your partner *wants* to go over threshold—for example, she might want to stop drinking coffee—and have her run that content through the threshold process. If she still wants to drink coffee when she's done, then you have missed something. In that case you need to find out what she has to do differently in order to go over threshold permanently.

Be careful when you pick the new content, to be *very* sure that your life will be better after you've crossed threshold. This pattern is typically irreversible. You don't want to ruin a happy relationship or make someone quit a job that he likes or needs to stay in. Not in this seminar! If you can't think of anything you want to cross threshold on, do not test.

Here are several guidelines that can make your task easier. There are usually three stages to the threshold pattern. Most people have some way of stacking examples, some way of saying "Never again" to those examples, and a very important third stage is to have some representation of a new life.

Although you will usually find those three stages, don't expect to find exactly what Bobbi does. We've never yet found two people who do it exactly the same way. There is a great deal of variation in exactly how examples stack, how crossing threshold actually happens, and what occurs afterwards, in terms of submodalities and representational systems. You might even have a partner who doesn't stack multiple examples in order to go over threshold, but instead uses some other way to build intensity, such as making a *single* example picture bigger and bigger.

As you gather information, keep in mind that this threshold pattern usually happens over time. You don't want to know everything that happened, only the changes in submodalities that relate to the transitions in the process of crossing threshold.

We'd like to give you one other example of someone going over threshold, so that you have an idea of the variety of ways people can do it. A man had been quite overweight and had tried all sorts of diets, pills and plans to lose weight, but nothing had worked. At a certain point in time he simply decided, "Never again. I'm not going to overeat like I used to." From then on, he had no trouble dieting, and very rapidly got down to a reasonable weight. He did this on his own one "thoughtful" evening; he didn't go to a therapist or anything. He called it "willpower," but in NLP we always ask, "What is the *structure* of his willpower?" If it can work for him, it can work for someone else. He made a series of pictures. First he saw himself the way he looked in the present—big and round. Then he made a picture of himself being a little bigger and rounder a few weeks in the future. He kept making these pictures of himself going farther and farther into the future, and getting bigger and bigger and rounder and rounder. In the last picture he saw himself lying dead like a beached whale, with his little daughter standing next to him looking very sad. When he saw this final picture of himself, a loud voice said, "No!" and he crossed threshold.

In this example, you can see the kind of stacking process that often occurs. The stacking part is an analogue change; he keeps stacking pictures until he reaches "critical mass"—in this case quite literally! At this point there is a digital change as well, the loud compelling voice saying, "No!" There will always be some kind of digital submodality change when someone actually crosses over threshold. With Bobbi, the "light-fiber" cord breaks and the picture blacks out.

Go ahead and do the exercise; it may take you a while. Find out if you can be done in a half-hour each.

Exercise Summary
1. Discover the analogue submodalities that shift in order to *reach* threshold.
2. Discover the digital submodality shifts that occur as you *cross* threshold and go "Never again."
3. Notice how you represent the new alternative life you will move toward. .

*　*　*　*　*

Discussion

OK, have you all had it up to here with this exercise? (laughter) Let's hear some examples of what you found.

Hank:　This may sound silly, but at one point in my life I decided never to eat hot dogs again.

OK, tell us exactly how you went over threshold with hot dogs.

Hank:　Well, in my office at the university, a group of us would always get together for the ''Twenty-five cent Friday Hot Dog Special'' at the Student Union. I would have one or two, and then half an hour later they would come back on me with a vengeance—upset stomach, gas, the works. I finally just got tired of it, and decided ''Never again!''

How, specifically, did you get to that point?

Hank:　I got a dissociated picture of myself—a color movie, as a matter of fact—experiencing the noxious aftereffects of those hot dogs. The movie started out fairly close, but as I watched it, it ''zoomed out'' until it got far enough away that I could see how stupid it was to go on eating those awful things. At that point, my own voice came in and said, ''That's just crazy. I'm never eating another hot dog again!'' And I never have.

Did you stack more than this one movie?

Hank:　No, I think it was the zooming out part that made the most difference. I finally got far enough away to see how ridiculous the situation was.

Did you cycle some new content through it?

Hank:　Yes. I need to sever my formal relationship with a group whose meetings I've been chairing. Because the relationship no longer addresses some of my major interests, I want to spend less time dealing with the group and more time working on my own projects. I've been thinking about leaving for some time, but haven't gotten around to it.

So what did you do?

Hank:　I got a movie of myself at one of their meetings, bored out of my skull, but still working to make sure everything was proceeding smoothly. I zoomed it out until I got to the point where I could see how useless it was for me to be there. At that point I said something like, ''The next meeting is my swan song!'' So my mind is made up: I'm out.

Good! Notice that for Hank, there isn't really any stacking of pictures; instead, the zooming out of the movie is the analogue part of reaching threshold. Then when it's far enough away, the digital voice comes in—"That's crazy! Never again!"

That exact method probably wouldn't work for many of you, but we know that Hank has identified all the necessary elements to make it work for him, because he successfully used it with a different content. In his case the submodality structure of the new alternative wasn't specified, but it's clearly there: other food in place of the hot dogs, and his own projects in place of the meeting.

Relationship to timelines and association/dissociation

Tom: When I reached threshold, I crashed through a pane of glass and became associated into the new activity. Actually, it was a sense of control and practical choice—knowing what to do, rather than a specific activity.

Tom is mentioning two very important parts of crossing threshold. Breaking through the pane of glass is a digital shift that allows him to associate with a representation that had previously been dissociated behind the glass. This representation of new activity is also a key element in the pattern.

Tom: The interesting thing is that when I tried it on another behavior that I wanted to stop, when I crashed through the pane of glass, I immediately became associated into the new possibility.

Bob: What's your memory of the old behavior?

Tom: Good question. (long pause as Tom looks to his left and slightly down) I don't have a memory of it.

Surely you know what it was. . . .

Tom: I'm sure I—Yeah, I can explain what the old behavior was, but as far as the submodalities, I can't seem to get it back.

And we know by watching Tom that he sees the old behavior to his left and slightly down. Do you remember Tom's timeline from yesterday? The old behavior is now in the past on Tom's timeline.

I happened to be watching Tom *before* he went over threshold; the behavior he wanted to stop was straight out in front of him, where the present is on his timeline. Now that he's gone over threshold, the old behavior has shifted into the past, down here on his timeline (gestures to Tom's left). It seems to have gotten smaller as well.

Sandy: Mine was kind of like that. I was thinking about when I became a non-smoker. Now smoking is so far in the past it's almost as if it was somebody else who smoked all those cigarettes. It's not even real.

This underscores several interesting points. One is the intersection between this method and the timeline. Before going over threshold, people usually see the old behavior in their present, and sometimes the future. After people have gone over threshold, that old behavior has usually shifted to the past on their timeline.

Association/dissociation is often a key, too. The way Sandy said, "It's almost as if it was somebody else," lets us know that she is now very dissociated from smoking. The old behavior usually becomes dissociated when people go over threshold. When you think about that old behavior after you're over threshold, you're dissociated from it.

The new representation may also change with respect to association/dissociation. Tom became associated into the new choices when he went over threshold. It doesn't work that way for everyone; some people stay dissociated from the new choices as in the swish. Since it's very often a key factor, when gathering information both about the old behavior and the image of new possibilities, we suggest asking, "Are you associated or dissociated?" This dimension often reverses when the person goes over threshold.

Ecology: Building an Alternative

I was pleased to notice that most of you were doing a great job of checking for ecology. You discovered that sometimes people need to make adjustments before going over threshold. Last year one person attempted to go over threshold with smoking, but didn't make it all the way through. However, putting the content of smoking into his threshold pattern was useful to him. He became aware of some positive things smoking did for him which made it unecological to quit until he had new choices for achieving those goals.

In some cases you may discover that you can't find a way to adjust the ecology so that a person feels comfortable going over threshold—it's just not appropriate. Some of you noticed this, and I congratulate you on not forcing the issue.

We can't overemphasize how important it is for the person going over threshold to have some representation of what else to do with his life. Most people aren't willing to go "Never again!" unless they have some representation of a new life. They need to know that they will have access to something new and better in the future before they eliminate the only choice they have now. Barbara's partners were trying to help her go over threshold on something, and it just wasn't working. She was going through the submodality changes they had identified, but she wasn't ready to say "Never again." I asked Barbara to build an image of her life without the response she wanted to eliminate. Once she had that, she went over threshold easily.

If somehow you managed to push someone over threshold *without* a new alternative, that person is very likely to become depressed, or even suicidal. A former alcoholic in one of our seminars described how she had gone over threshold spontaneously with alcohol, *without* having a new alternative. She felt very suicidal and literally remained in bed for three days, until she began to develop a representation of how it was possible for her to live without alcohol. When someone is suicidal, or speaks of having no future, often this is what has happened. That dangerous phase can be bypassed if you make absolutely sure the person has a representation of a workable alternative life *before* going over threshold.

Leah: How would you use the threshold pattern for an alcoholic?

What are the consequences of drinking that are unpleasant? Find out how the person goes over threshold, and stack those consequences of drinking in the same way. How many more mornings are you willing to endure that splitting headache, or the fear that you may have done something awful while you were drunk the night before? This pattern can work for *anything*, if you make it subjectively compelling.

Sam: With something as pervasive as drinking, I'm curious about how you would represent the future life without alcohol. That sounds like a negative outcome.

Good point. I might start by saying "the future without drinking," but then I'd ask, "What *else* are you doing?" Since I don't know what else they want to be doing, I don't want to put in anything specific at the beginning.

Keep in mind that you'd probably use this pattern along with a lot of other NLP tools. This method presupposes a lot of behavioral choice— that they'll be able to handle themselves without the alcohol. You may need to *first* use a lot of other methods to build behavioral choices into the future.

Stacking into the future

Jerry: When we elicited my threshold pattern, I noticed that I saw a long string of examples of the situation in the past. I scanned that long movie screen of how things had been. It wasn't until I put in the new content that I realized that I had to add on a screen that went on into my future, and project the same pattern into the future. I knew things had been like that in the past, and I didn't like it. But I didn't get fed up enough with it until I saw my life that way in the future.

That's quite common. For a lot of people, it's not just stacking in the past; after a certain point, the person thinks, "Wait a minute. Life could go on this way until death. And this looks too disgusting for me to continue." Stacking into the future speeds up the process and also saves you a lot of wear and tear; you'll get out of a bad situation a lot sooner. The woman who was slapped on the first date stacked almost completely into the future.

Ralph: I did that when I got a divorce. Right when I went over threshold, I saw myself with my wife, with bad things happening, on into the future for the rest of my life. I didn't like it, so I made up my mind to do something about it.

Specifying a Digital Outcome

Al: We didn't know what to do because my partner wants to lose weight, but it obviously wouldn't work to have her say, "Never again" to eating.

I'm glad you noticed that, or she would be in big trouble! So what is it that she *does* want to say "Never again" about? She doesn't want to quit eating. Perhaps she wants to never again *over*eat. If you help her change the frame to *overeating*, she'll be working with something digital that she can be comfortable saying "Never again!" to. When you use this pattern, be sure the person is describing the behavior in such a way that she *can* and *wants* to say "Never again" to it.

Al: Eating is something she'll have to confront at least three times a day. Isn't it likely that sometime she'll overeat?

That's possible. I'm sure you all know stories about people who go on diets and do fine until that fateful day when they pig out once on ice cream, or cookies, or crackers, or whatever. Or maybe they eat one twinkie, and suddenly they think the whole diet is destroyed! Weeks of dieting are ruined, and they *know* they've failed, right? In situations like this, it's useful to build in possible exceptions, so that it's not a sign of absolute failure if they backslide once or twice; they can wipe the crumbs off their lips and get back to dieting.

Cathy: Can you just take the final submodalities for the old behavior and map the new behavior across into that?

I haven't tried that, but my guess is that your success rate will be much higher if you put the person through the whole process. If you put the person through their threshold process, those ending submodalities happen naturally. If you just tried to install those final submodalities, my guess is that you'll get a lot of resistance. You'll also be less apt to notice any ecology problems.

Man: Isn't the threshold pattern another way of changing criteria?

The threshold pattern doesn't change criteria; it *utilizes* them. If you see only one or a few minor examples, that may violate your criteria, but not enough for you to take action. When you see many, many minor examples occurring over time, or one major example, it violates those *same* criteria, but *more so*, so that you go over threshold.

Using the Threshold Process "Unconsciously"

Once you really understand how this pattern works, and you have good sensory acuity, you can put someone through the pattern without overtly getting all the details of what she did in her brain to go over threshold.

I did this with Lou during the exercise. She had a good example of having crossed threshold in the past, but she couldn't identify her submodalities for going over threshold. I asked her to put herself back through the experience of crossing threshold. I wanted her to start at the beginning of the threshold process, and then reexperience what it was like to go over threshold. As Lou began, she nodded her head in a particular way, and she made a certain hand gesture that I later "stole" to anchor the whole process. I watched Lou's nonverbals as she reexperienced going over threshold, and mentioned that as she did this she was not only remembering, but *her brain was learning the pathway that she already had for going over threshold*. When Lou finished going through the experience once, I asked her to do it again, *so that her brain could really memorize the sequence for easily and ecologically crossing threshold.* This time I utilized my anchor to help her get right back into the beginning of the process, and I observed the same sequence of nonverbal shifts as she went through it. After two "rehearsals," I asked Lou to take the new content that she wanted to go over threshold with, and put it through the same process. I told her that even if she didn't consciously know all the detailed steps, her brain knew what to do. I also used my nonverbal anchors to make sure that her brain started on the right track.

This way of doing it isn't as dependable as a thorough knowledge of the sequence of submodality changes the person goes through. If the "unconscious" approach doesn't quite work, you'll need to go back and troubleshoot to find out exactly what to do. However it's nice to have another choice, especially when you need to do more covert work.

Motivation

Richard: Could you do this in the opposite direction? Could you use this pattern to get yourself to *start exercising* rather than to *stop overeating*?

If you want to *start* doing something, you need to create motivation, and it's simplest to "map across" to something that you are motivated to do, or create a compelling future.

In contrast, the last straw threshold is for *breaking* a motivation that is *already* established. You're already motivated to have the car, or the habit, or the relationship, but it's not working the way you wanted it to. As with the compulsion blowout, it's not possible to just destack; something has to build to an irreversible threshold.

Kate: Are there people who don't have any way to cross threshold? People who stay in really bad situations no matter what?

Yes, there are. If you don't have a way of going over threshold, you might consider adding one to your repertoire. Some people never learned how to stack experiences over time. Typically they wait until someone *else* goes over threshold and ends a situation. Since they never go over threshold and take decisive action, they are often given a psychiatric label such as "passive-agressive" just because they don't have a particular skill. If someone is in a situation where they keep getting abused, or putting up with something that's not worth putting up with, it may be that they don't know how to stack.

Another possibility is that they do recognize that there are many unpleasant examples in the past, but they think the future will be better. The wife of the alcoholic thinks, "Well, I'll change him," or "He'll do better in the future, so I'll stay with him." Sometimes having them put the examples in their future as well as their past gets them over threshold. This is what Jerry did.

· A third possibility is that the person recognizes that their horrible life will continue, but he can't see any alternative. Sometimes when you build a subjectively real alternative, the person will go over threshold automatically, because the lack of an alternative was all that held him back. On the other hand, sometimes using this pattern after you've used other techniques to build an alternative new life is what locks the change in.

The other extreme is the person who goes over threshold at the drop of a hat. This person may have many ex-friends and ex-jobs. Sometimes it's useful to learn to go over threshold on a certain activity, rather than eliminate an entire relationship. You can decide never again to trust someone with money, but realize that you can still trust him with secrets, or with property, and keep him as a friend.

Crossing threshold is a very powerful pattern, one that can result in major life changes. However, we urge you to think of it as a "pattern of last resort." Often much simpler and more basic NLP patterns will get the outcomes your clients want, with far fewer possible repercussions or side-effects.

VII

Internal/External Reference

Some people frequently get into difficulties because they assume that others are right, and base their decisions on others' opinions. Sociologists have described these people as "other-directed" or "conformists." NLP describes such people as using an "external reference." *External reference* means that somebody or something *else* decides for me what is good, bad, right, wrong, fun, boring, or whatever. Someone with an external reference might repeatedly ask others what to do, or say, "Let me check my horoscope to find out what to do." Therapists are often the external reference for clients: "Dr. X says I have an Oedipus complex, so I must," or "If he will just tell me how to live my life, then I can be happy." One of our favorite cartoons shows a psychiatrist saying to a patient on the couch, "I have good news for you, Mr. Jones; my mother thinks you're getting much better." If an externally-referenced person has several different people giving him directions, he'll typically have difficulty choosing among them. People who get into religious cults usually have a single external reference—the cult leader, or whatever scriptures are used as the exclusive basis for making decisions.

In contrast, *internal reference* means that *I* decide what's right, wrong, and so on. I may take in lots of information from other people or from the environment, but I am the one who decides about it.

Woman: So does internal mean you pay attention to your internal experience, and external mean you pay attention to what's outside?

No. I'm glad you raised that question, because that's a different distinction. You're talking about the difference between external and internal *awareness*. *Reference* doesn't necessarily have to do with where your

133

attention is, it has to do with who decides. I can have an internal reference, and still listen to the opinions of others around me or gather lots of information from the outside. But if I have an internal reference, I am using my own judgement to decide about all these opinions and data.

Many people use internal/external reference as a diagnostic category— are you an internal reference person or an external reference person? We've been exploring the submodality differences between internal and external reference, so that you can *change* what you do, if you want to.

Group Exercise

We'd like you all to experiment with us to find out what happens in *your* brain when you go from internal to external reference, or vice versa. We want you all to pretend to have an internal reference, and then pretend to have an external reference, and discover how your submodalities shift for those two experiences. You can all probably think of times when you were more internal or more external in your reference. For now, we want you to pretend to do each one to an extreme. If there are some of you who have difficulty going to an extreme of internal or external reference, that's also interesting information.

First, we want you to pretend to have an internal reference. I'm going to say something to you, and since you have an internal reference system, *you're* the one who decides or evaluates what I say: "If you stand on your head facing north for one half hour each day, this will greatly improve the quality of your life." Notice what your experience is as you consider that with an internal reference—*you* decide. . . .

Now, temporarily pretend that you have an external reference, and I'm it. Keep in mind that this is only temporary; you will easily get back your own ability to decide as soon as you've tried this. For now, I'm your external reference. You know ahead of time that whatever I say is true. "If you hum middle C each morning for a minimum of five minutes, this will put you in greater harmony with the universe." Notice your experience as you respond to this statement with an external reference.

Discussion

So what shifted? What is different when you go from internal to external reference?

Dee: When I did external reference, there was only one voice— yours. With internal reference, there were two or more voices; it was more like a dialogue, or a discussion. I heard your voice, and mine, too.

That's fairly typical. What about pictures? What changed for you with pictures?

Dee: It was the same with pictures; there was only one for external reference, and more than one for internal refernce.

Dick: For internal reference I got multiple pictures. One would be of what the other person was saying, but I also made a bunch of other pictures related to my *own* experience: what I know from the past, or what I can make up, or whatever—alternative possible choices to decide among.

That's an essential part of the way most people are able to have an internal reference.

Carolyn: I don't have multiple pictures for internal. I make an associated movie and run it for a few minutes, so I'll know if I want to do it or not. As the movie's running, I ask myself questions about what's going on: "Is this doing me any good? How much do I like this person? Should I do this for them? Is there anything they have that I want?"

How do you answer those questions, verbally or visually?

Carolyn: Verbally. "No, this isn't fun; I don't want to do this."

That's another way to begin to develop many alternatives, so that you can decide what you like best. How do you do external reference?

Carolyn: I still have a movie, but I stay dissociated. I don't test it to see whether I want it or not.

Ann: In external reference, the picture of what the other person was saying was overwhelmingly close. For internal reference, the pictures were much farther away.

Most people have a big, bright, close picture for external reference. That makes sense when you think about it; if you're responding to someone else, and you make the picture of what they're telling you really big and close, there won't be any room for *your* pictures of other alternatives. It's pretty hard to think for yourself if all you can see on the inside is a representation of what the "expert" says.

Now check the location of your images. Is there a difference between how high up you see the images when doing internal or external reference?

Sam: External was higher.

A lot of you are nodding. Were there any exceptions to that? . . . So, Joan, your representation of what the other person said was lower in external reference? Was it more compelling to you that way?

Joan: No. It was lower, and it was smaller, and dimmer, and I was very small in the picture. For internal the picture was higher up and a lot bigger.

That's puzzling; it doesn't seem to fit the pattern of the other responses so far.

Chris: Mine was fairly similar to that. But I realized that when I tried to do external, I was actually taking an internal stance, a meta-position. That's why the picture is small and low. I had trouble really being external. Then Richard and I sort of thought—we both said it together—"We can do this if we age-regress." I regressed back to childhood, and immediately the external was big and glowing—somebody picking me up.

Does what Chris said fit for you, Joan?

Joan: Yes, it does. It was very hard for me to do external reference, except briefly.

So those apparent exceptions make some sense after all. They always do, when you get enough information.

Fran: In our group, we all experienced more relaxation in external. It felt like a relief to just wait to be told what to do, and not have to make decisions.

Bill: We had just the reverse. Our group must have been more internally-oriented. We all felt a lot of tension in dealing with the external authority; it felt like a battle: "I hate this."

So your natural tendency felt most comfortable. It makes sense that you would feel tension if you're fighting what the other person is saying.

Sally: I had trouble doing the external reference. If I thought something sounded like a command, a door slammed shut in my brain, and I stopped listening. Sandy was more flexible; she could take in what was being told to her and consider it, and go on to other pictures that were alternatives. But I couldn't even get that far. When I think another person is eliminating my choices, I say "Forget it!"

That kind of protective polarity response can be useful, but because it's such an all-or-nothing reaction, there's also some risk involved. What if somebody shouts "Fire! Get out of the building NOW!" and you stand there thinking, "No way—you can't tell *me* what to do!" (laughter) A polarity response like this has the *intent* of protecting you from the opinions of others and preserving your range of choices, but it often actually results in *limiting* your choices.

No matter what someone tells me—whether it is a command, praise, flattery, criticism, or whatever—I would rather be open to the content and be able to evaluate it for myself instead of slamming the door on it and limiting my choices: "I don't like the sound of that, so forget it!" If I react that way to someone's voice tone, I can lose important information. I like to have the flexibility to keep my options open, to listen to ideas—

however they're delivered, no matter how crazy they may seem. What I've just said is an example of internal reference, and it also has a couple of reframing patterns in it.

Characteristics of External Reference

Now let's draw some generalizations from all this data. If you want to develop a strong *external* reference, make big, bright, close pictures of what an expert says. Be sure this image is large and compelling enough so that there's no room in your visual field for any thoughts of your own. When you see these other people in your mind's eye, see them slightly elevated above you. If you hear anything, make it the "expert's" voice, or your own voice repeating what the expert says, preferably using the expert's tone and tempo.

Installing External Reference

Leaders are great at installing external reference, so you'll do what they say. They make sure that they're standing up on high platforms when they talk; you certainly don't usually see them in positions lower than the audience. They often put up larger-than-life posters of themselves looking down on people. We know of one seminar leader who puts a larger-than-life poster of himself behind him when he trains, and also has two huge TV monitors with close-ups of his face on either side.

Cult leaders also do a lot to discourage followers from thinking of other possibilities. At one open meeting we attended, a young man asked a very reasonable (to us) question of a well-known guru. The guru responded by saying solemnly, "I am a wood carver; you are a piece of wood. Last month a student decided not to do what I said; the next day he was in a car wreck and died."

Greg: It sounds a lot like the military!

Frank: You mean the military *isn't* a cult? (laughter) I always thought of it as the same thing.

It's no accident that the military much prefers younger recruits, most of whom haven't yet been able to develop a strong internal reference. Although we're no great fans of the military, it's often true that the survival of a military unit depends on instant and unquestioning obedience to orders. Hopefully the guy who's giving orders knows more than you do, and knows what he's doing, but even if he doesn't, it's probably better to follow his orders than act as an isolated individual.

Chris: Another thing I tried was very revealing to me. I took on the external reference and then imagined I was receiving some instructions that either were confusing or that I didn't understand. It was a very disconcerting experience. I got this big, bright, close picture but it was all fuzzy.

Right. If you're assuming someone else is right, and then they give you a bunch of confusing gobbledegook, you'll probably assume that you received adequate instructions but you can't understand what to do. That can be very difficult.

Sandy: It's like what often happens to little kids in school. The teacher's the authority, so she's supposed to know. And she gives the kids confusing instructions and then they don't know what to do. That's got to be one reason a lot of kids do poorly in school.

Andy: I was looking around the room when you had us do the exercise, and I noticed that everyone's posture really shifted when we went from external reference to internal. For external, people were leaning forward more and for internal most people leaned back a bit.

Good observation. For external reference, people are also more apt to tilt their heads up and have a wide-eyed look; for internal, the head typically moves back and the eyelids are less open.

When to Do What

In most situations, you do better if you have an internal reference, so that you can make your own decisions according to your own values and the best information you have. Internal reference is also often strongly correlated with survival. Victor Frankl discovered that many survivors of concentration camps were able to maintain their *internal* choice, even in situations that were seemingly totally controlled by others. Survivors of cancer, too, often internally create alternatives in their lives rather than passively accept the sentence that's been handed down to them. The "experts" tell them they'll die in 6 months, and they disagree. If this is possible for people in such desperate circumstances, how much more is possible for us?

However, in cases where someone else really *does* know more than you do, an external reference will work better. For example, if you take a sick child to the emergency room, it makes sense to rely on the judgement of the emergency room physician, rather than take the time to become a doctor so that you can decide for yourself.

At times like these, your own information is so incomplete that it is appropriate to accept someone else as an external reference for a particular context, at least temporarily. Most people do this whenever they go to a doctor, a plumber, or any other person who is an expert at something they know very little about. When you do this, having an external reference is carefully contextualized, and is *nested within* an internal reference, integrating the two. You are still carefully deciding when it's useful to trust someone else's opinion, and you can still apply any tests that your minimal knowledge permits. If your doctor tells you to use leeches, or your plumber suggests a topless cesspool in your living room, you may decide to find another expert!

Jose: One way I will accept an external reference is if I look at what someone is saying and I don't have anything else to compare it to, because I don't know anything about it. The other way is if I look at what this person has said in the past, and he was usually right.

Those are both examples of nesting external within internal.

Creating an Internal Reference

Many people would like to get better at deciding for themselves, rather than being swayed by the opinions of others. If you want to have a strong *internal* reference, make sure that you have ways to generate alternative representations, either by an internal search or an external search, or both. These alternative internal representations should be at least as compelling as the representations derived from other people.

If you'd like to have more of an internal reference, think of a situation when you have been more external than you'd like; for example you followed someone's advice, and it didn't work out well. You can go back to that time and take the representation of what the other person is saying and shrink it down, move it farther away, or make it dimmer and less colorful, etc. Then you'll respond to it less, and have more room for making your *own* alternative representations. You can also explore that past event for early evidence that it wasn't a good idea to trust this person, or for missed opportunities for you to apply tests that would have given you this information. Then future-pace what you have learned.

Becoming "Unintimidated" by Authority Figures

We've used this technique with people who are intimidated by authority figures. When the client thinks of the person who intimidates him, he typically says something like, "Oh, yeah, I can see him. The picture is big and bright and close, and it's kind of high up." In this case, we ask him to make the picture smaller, move it back a bit, lower it, and turn down the brightness. This allows him to think about someone in authority without being overwhelmed and having to necessarily agree with what he says. It becomes easier to treat the other person like a peer instead of Big Brother.

You might also need to explicitly install a protective voice like Carolyn has, that repeatedly questions what someone else is saying in terms of her outcomes, examines the consequences of doing what someone says, and suggests alternative possibilities. If someone has only *one* representation of a situation, he may act on it even if you make it small and dim and far away. In the next chapter we describe a specific method for teaching people how to make their own evaluations and decisions.

Other-Responders

Some people aren't particularly intimidated by authority figures, but are overly-responsive to the needs of others, while neglecting their own. This often results in "burnout," and it usually has a similar structure to intimidation. To become overly-responsive to the needs of others, first make a representaion of what that person needs. Then either make that image big, bright, and close, or zoom in and make it panoramic, so that it fills up your visual screen and you have no room for pictures of what you want. If all you can see is others' needs, that is what you will respond to. These pictures are usually *not* higher up, as they are with intimidation.

For the antidote:

1. Think of someone to whom you over-respond, denying your own needs.

2. Notice how you see this person in your mind's eye. Is the picture large and close, perhaps panoramic? Does their voice have some quality that makes it impossible to ignore? (If you have trouble identifying the important submodalities, *contrast* this image with an image of someone you don't feel over-responsive to.)

3. Move that picture of them/their needs further away and make it smaller, dimmer, less colorful, etc. If it started out panoramic, reduce the panorama to a small framed picture in front of you. Let their voice fade in volume or change tonality in a useful way, until you feel less overwhelmed by this person's needs.

4. Now make another screen the same size, brightness, and distance from you as the picture of the other person's needs. Ask yourself, "What do *I* want?" and put your answers in this new frame.

5. Now you are looking at two screens: one represents your wants, and one represents the other person's wants. Ask yourself, "What would best meet the needs/desires of *both* me and this other person?" In certain contexts, or with certain people, it may be more appropriate to make your

own needs more (or less) important than the other's. Are you better able to respond to both, in appropriate balance?

6. Future-pace your chosen way of seeing things into the appropriate future situations.

When someone is externally-referenced, it's relatively easy to help him become more internal. Most people who voluntarily seek help are those with more external reference. Of course, they may have less conscious parts that have other ideas! People who are very external will tend to ask you what to do and then follow all your directions, because they assume you're right. Since it's usually not too hard to get them to accept *you* as their external reference, you can simply tell them what to do: "I think it's unquestionable that you should pay more attention to your own desires and think for yourself." If the person does that, she will start developing more internal reference. If she refuses to do what you ask, she will *also* be acting out of a more internal reference—deciding for herself, instead of doing what others say.

Feedback

If people with an internal reference are open and receptive to feedback and information from the outside, they and those around them are probably happy. If you want to become more receptive to the views of others, and utilize input better, you can make your own ideas less compelling (smaller, dimmer, farther away), making room for other representations. You can make others' ideas at least compelling enough to make you consider them.

If someone is only a little oblivious to feedback, ask him if he has any other people in his pictures when he makes decisions. Probably he doesn't. Ask him to add in wife, children, employer, and any other people who will be affected by his decisions, and then ask him to pay attention to how these other people respond to a proposed decision or action. This will cause a useful shift toward noticing feedback. Strictly speaking, this is a *content* intervention rather than a submodality *process* intervention, but it's very useful for helping someone become more external. Someone who is externally-referenced is more likely to already have lots of other people in his pictures. Some have a cast of thousands! It may be useful for them to experiment with making decisions without having quite so many onlookers.

Some people with an internal reference go to an extreme: they assume ahead of time that they are right, and disregard others' opinions. These people are usually making such compelling images of their own opinions that there is no room for even considering alternate representations. When someone is closed to feedback, it's likely to be much more difficult to get her to change, because she is already preprogrammed to disregard other's ideas—including yours!

Someone with a strong internal reference rarely seeks help; he is more likely to be a court referral or an uncooperative spouse. When working with someone who is closed to feedback, you have to be very careful to pace his belief system, and part of that is that he is right and you are wrong. "You obviously know far more about your situation than I could ever learn; the most I can do is offer some poor suggestions in the faint hope that you might decide that one or two might possibly be useful to you." Anything you want him to do should be framed as much as possible as *his* idea, or at least as *his* decision. "You have already told me how important this is to you. Here are a couple of other ideas for you to consider—which you have undoubtedly already thought of before—that might make your plans even more complete." By pacing the person's belief that you have nothing worth listening to, you paradoxically become worth listening to.

If a person is totally closed to feedback, that's probably more dangerous—especially to others—than being too external. Think of people you know who might fit this category. These are the people who think, "I don't have to see or hear anything from outside to know I'm right." These people don't look to the outside world for relevant information: refinements, dis confirmations, additional learnings, etc. They don't hear feedback either, even when it's offered, because they're usually telling themselves, "I already know I'm right, so why bother?" Shifting this kind of extreme internal reference is very difficult, because the instant you say anything that violates what he *knows* to be true, he'll go, "No way!" Working with this type of person is a real challenge, because he lives in a very narrow and specific reality. A paranoid person is a prime example of this.

Sally: How do you get around that?

Well, there aren't any foolproof methods, but there are a number of things you can try, most of which are covert.

With a paranoid, or anyone else who is mistrustful, you can say, "Don't trust me! Even though I don't want to harm you, I might do so accidentally. I want you to be very vigilant, and carefully examine everything I say and do, to be sure that *what we do here together is for your benefit*." Again, by instructing the person to distrust you—which he is going to do anyway— you paradoxically become trustworthy. As you do this, you can slip in a number of presuppositions and reframes that will be useful later. For instance, the three sentences in quotes above introduce the distinctions between intention, behavior, and outcome, as well as the presuppositions that it's possible to work together and that this can benefit the person.

Rather than trying to change a person's belief system, it's often much easier to use it as leverage to get him to do what you want. After pacing thoroughly, you can use all your other NLP tools, as long as they are covert, or appropriately framed. "Since you're so much more intelligent than the rest of your family, it should be very simple and easy for you to be kind and gentle with them as they slowly learn what you already know." "Since you're so certain that you are right, there could be no harm in listening carefully to your wife's opinions and thoughtfully considering them as if they were as important as your own. Only someone who was insecure about his own views would be unwilling to do that."

Someone who is closed to feedback will usually agree that it's dangerous to trust others. After pacing this, you can point out that others will often act stupidly in ways that could harm him, so it's important to know what they're thinking—no matter how misguided it is. From there it's only a small step to point out the importance of considering others' thinking in making his own decisions. It's even more useful to *demonstrate* how being closed to feedback can be dangerous to him. You can do this with an example from his past difficulties, or with a present example in a couple or family session, or you can create such a situation yourself.

Another alternative is to bypass the person's conscious mind completely by using metaphor and hypnotic language patterns to appeal to ignored and less conscious parts of the person.

Sometimes you can learn enough about the person's belief system to pace it thoroughly and then "accidentally," ruin it by pointing out inconsistencies or contradictions, or by sincere requests to clear up your confusion. However, be very cautious if you try this. If you fail, you will lose rapport—possibly forever—and if you succeed in ruining his reality, he may get pretty strange.

Our favorite story about this is about a mental patient in the V.A. Hospital in Palo Alto who believed he was God. He was very aloof and distant, and no one had been able to make contact with him. Don Jackson, a *very* hip psychologist, offered to demonstrate how to get through to him. When the patient was brought in, he was offered a chair next to Jackson. He takes the chair and moves it far away, and then sits down with a regal flair, and looks at the group silently with an air of immense superiority and disdain.

After observing him for several minutes, Don Jackson goes over to him, kneels before him deferentially, bows his head, and says, "Obviously you are God. Since you are God, only you deserve the keys to this hospital,'' and places his ring of hospital keys gently in the patient's lap. He pauses, and then says slowly, ''However, if you are God, you have no need for these keys.'' Then he stands up and walks back to his chair and sits down. The patient sits there percolating for a few minutes, quite agitated, and then jumps up, pulls his chair over to Jackson, sits down, looks intently into his eyes and says emphatically, ''Man, *one* of us is *crazy!*''

Don Jackson's communication, both verbal and nonverbal, paced the patient's world and then pointed out a contradiction in it. That patient *could* have replied, ''Although I don't need the keys, since I'm God, I'll take them anyway,'' but he *didn't.*

John Rosen does the same thing a little less subtly. With a patient who believes he's God, John will get four or five powerful assistants, wrestle the patient to the floor, sit on his chest, and then say, ''If you're God, how come we ordinary mortals can pin you to the floor? You're totally helpless. If you're God, go ahead and destroy us.'' Rosen insists on contact; it's very hard to be catatonic when someone's sitting on your chest and shouting at you. If the patient turns his head away, Rosen will grab his head and turn it back, and if he closes his eyes, Rosen will open them! He's also willing to continue this for many hours, if necessary. That may seem crude, but it's also pretty hard for the patient to ignore.

Richard: I've found that some people with strong internal reference also have strong polarity responses.

That's a good point. Sometimes you can use that as leverage: ''Well, of course someone like *you* could *never* learn to demonstrate your intelligence by accommodating to other people who are important to you.''

The extremes of internal and external reference are interesting, and the contrasts between them can teach you some useful distinctions. Of course, most people fall somewhere between the extremes; they have some way to generate alternatives to what someone else says, and some way to compare and evaluate them. Internal or external reference is a function of the submodalities a person uses to construct alternative representations. You can often assist him in finding a better way to achieve his outcomes by asking him to experiment with adjusting these representations.

In closing we want to warn you about another way of nesting reference that is less obvious, and much less useful. You can have an external reference and nest internal reference within it! Many cult leaders seem to have an internal reference: they tell others what to do. However, this is embedded in an external reference: a desperate need to have a large group of followers who agree with them. Since this system is so circular—the only important aspect of the belief is that a number of other people also believe it—it is also much more fragile. If the followers leave, the leader's world collapses. Jim Jones is a prime example, and there are many others—even some within the little world of NLP. Peter Goblen said it well in the following poem,

Pusher

Beware the seeker of disciples
the missionary
the pusher
all proselytizing men
all who claim they have found
the path to heaven.

For the sound of their words
is the silence of their doubt.

The allegory of your conversion
sustains them through their uncertainty.

Persuading you, they struggle
to persuade themselves.

They need you
as they say you need them:
there is a symmetry they do not mention
in their sermon
or in the meeting
near the secret door.

As you suspect each one of them
be wary also of these words,
for I, dissuading you,
obtain new evidence
that there is no shortcut,
no path at all,
no destination.

From *Journey Through the Light* © 1973 by Peter Goblen. Koheleth Publishing Co. San Francisco, CA.

VIII

A Strategy for Responding to Criticism

One of the fundamental presuppositions of NLP is that "There is no such thing as failure, only feedback." That's a nice thought, and it points in a very useful direction. However, for a majority of people it's just a cute sentence that doesn't automatically change their experience or response. Most people (roughly 70%) respond to criticism with immediate overwhelming bad feelings. Then they try to climb out of the emotional hole they have just dug for themselves by rationalizing, *trying* to access a good state, *trying* to be objective, etc. Since they are already in a bad state, usually none of these attempts work very well. And since most of their efforts are directed at regaining a good state, they typically do not make good use of any feedback information contained in the criticism. If they do make use of this information, it's usually much later.

At the other extreme, some people (perhaps 20%) respond to criticism by simply rejecting it. They protect themselves from any bad feelings, but they also prevent themselves from even considering whether any part of the criticism they receive is valid or useful feedback.

A third group (less than 10%) can listen to criticism without immediately feeling bad. They can also carefully consider whether the criticism contains useful feedback, and use that feedback in a productive way to modify their future behavior.

Of course these three groups aren't rigid categories. You can probably find an example of each of these patterns in your own life, depending upon your state of mind, the context, the criticizer, the frame, etc. Most of us occasionally get into bad states in which we respond unpleasantly to the most innocuous comment. Most of us also have times when we're in such

147

a good state that no matter how harshly we're criticized we can process it simply as interesting information.

Several years ago we became curious about the internal structure that allowed the ''experts'' at responding well to criticism to do it with such ease. We have modeled a number of people who are characteristically very good at responding to criticism in a useful way. While there are slight variations, all of them use the same basic internal process, and this strategy can be easily and quickly taught to others.

Example
(The following transcript is edited from a videotape of Steve demonstrating how to install this strategy in Carl, a participant in one of our Practitioner Certification Trainings in January, 1987. We also include some follow-up comments from Carl two weeks later. This demonstration and some additional discussion is available on a videotape: See Appendix I.)

We are going to do two things as I demonstrate this. One, I am going to demonstrate installing the strategy itself, and going through the different forks of the strategy and so on. The other thing I am going to do is demonstrate a sneaky way of installing a strategy, and that is by doing it in a dissociated state. And that is going to be kind of a trip for you, Carl, because you are not that hip on dissociation, are you?

Carl: Um, no, I like doing dissociation.

Can you do that? (Umhm.) OK. Great. So what I want you to do is see Carl out here in some situation in which someone might give him some kind of feedback which could be construed as criticism. You just see it out there, OK? (Carl leans back a little.) There you go! That's better. Good. You can see him as far away as you want. You can put a sheet of plexiglas here if you want. (Carl smiles and nods.) Oh, you like that one, don't you? OK, good. And I want you to stay in this dissociated state. What you are going to do is watch *him* go through this strategy. So you are just going to be an observer, and your function as an observer is to note at any time if any kind of problems come up with *him* out there. Then you can let me know about those and then we can do something to make it right. (OK.)

OK, great. So you are just going to watch this. And another way of framing this for people is that we are just going to try it out, out here, and we are not going to install it in him until it is all done, and it is totally OK out here; we are not going to do anything to him in here. Now in a way that is a bit of a scam. But it is a really useful scam with some people who are really wary: ''Nnnehh, don't meddle with my brain,'' or something like that. In one sense it's true that it will not be installed until and unless any ecological concerns have been dealt with. So that part of it is true. However, when you are seeing yourself out here going through it, you are also learning by self-metaphor inside. So this is the you that is going to learn a new way of responding to criticism, because I guess you are not too happy with the one you've got right now. Is that right?

Carl: (shaking head) No way, Jose. I don't like it.

OK, good. So see him out there, and in a moment someone else is going to say something which could be construed as criticism. And what *he* is gong to do is something very, very important. *He* is going to dissociate from the criticism. (OK.) So you are going to watch him— (*Carl:*   Dissociate, while I am dissociated.) While you are dissociated, right. (Oh, OK.)

It is sort of like the phobia procedure, where you have a three-place dissociation, and the function is the same. So someone is going to say something to Carl. And you can just make it up, what somebody might come over and say to him. And that Carl over there is going to keep this away somehow, (OK.) until he has had a chance to completely evaluate it. Now there are a couple of ways that he can do it. He can hear the words and imagine them printed out in space at arm's length. Or he can listen to them, but at a distance. (OK.)

And he can do that in several different ways and you can just watch and see how he does that. So, watch him as he hears the criticism. And it is some kind of criticism about him. And he is going to keep that sort of at arm's length. He is going to stay dissociated from it. And he is going to then make a picture of whatever that criticism is, preferably a movie. So he is going to make a representation of the criticism, dissociated. (OK.) And then he is going to compare that movie with a movie of whatever best information *he* has about that same situation. Is that clear? (Yeah.) OK. To evaluate it and say, "Well, does that make sense?" Is there some way that he can make sense out of that? Now, as you watch him do that, can he make some understanding of that? Does it make sense that someone could have said that about him?

Carl: It makes a *lot* of sense.

OK, it makes a *lot* of sense. At this point I want you to watch him decide on what kind of response he wants to make to that information. Because if it makes sense, that means it is good information that he didn't have before, right? (Yeah.) So he might say, "Thank you," or "Boy, I'm glad you brought that to my attention. I'll see what I can do about that." Or whatever.

Carl: Already he doesn't feel like shit inside. I mean—(laughter).
That's a good plan.
Carl: It just feels a whole lot better.

OK. And it is going to be easier for him now to make good use of whatever information is there because he doesn't feel like shit inside, right?

Carl: Right! Right. It is a whole lot easier for him to be objective about it.

Exactly. That is what "objective" is, by the way. "Objective" means you are dissociated. So, as you watch him, I want you to notice him go through the process of deciding what kind of response is appropriate to this situation, in terms of what he might do differently in the future; some kind of changes that he might decide he wants to go through, or whatever would be appropriate, a useful response to this information that has just been given to him. . . . OK, so he has gone through the decision process. And now have him actually carry that out, if it is appropriate to do that now and respond to this. Somebody criticized him, right? So if there is an appropriate response to this person like, "Thank you for bringing this to my attention," or "Boy, I screwed up," or—

Carl: Yeah! That's exactly what he did. He thanks the person!

That's a new one, huh? Instead of punching him out.

Carl: Yeah. He never thanked him before. In the past it wasn't so much anger towards the person, it was just anger towards himself (OK, all right), and he doesn't have to feel angry at himself any more. He can accept it as learning.

Great. And when he has completed that interaction with that person, I want you to watch him as he takes the time to future-pace doing something different in the future. So he has made some decisions about what he missed, or he didn't notice, or he was careless, or whatever it was. (Right.) How can he future-pace a new behavior? He might have to decide on a new behavior first. What is he going to do differently in the future, as you watch him future-pace that—so he goes through the decision *when* and *where* does he want to be different, and *how, specifically.* You might quickly run through some old responses or use the "New Behavior Generator," or whatever. OK. Has he done that change already? (Yeah.) OK.

Carl: Really, yeah. He doesn't feel the tension inside. He is glad the whole thing happened in the first place, because he is learning from it.

Is this a little different than your past experiences?

Carl: He has never experienced that in his life. Never!

It looks like it, doesn't it? (laughter) It looks like he just saw an angel come down out of the sky!

Carl: It is best, you know, and the context is with family, and—he just has not had an easy time with family before, but this is just—I mean, he is actually smiling.

OK. I would like you to run through a different scenario, a little bit different. So again you see him out here and nobody's around yet. (OK.) And this time, somebody's going to come up and either give a very vague criticism like "You skunk," or "You turkey," or something like that, so that he has to actually pause and gather information—because he hears "You turkey" and he makes a picture of a turkey and he makes a picture of himself and they don't match, right? (laughter) So he is going to have to gather information like, "Well, can you tell me more? How, specifically, am I a turkey?" or whatever, until he gets the information: "What is this person really commenting on?"

Carl: "What are they trying to tell him?"

"What are they trying to tell him?" And he can do this in a fairly polite, neutral way because he is just—

Carl: He can dissociate.

Dissociate. And he just wants to have the information. And when he has got sufficient information that he can make a movie of what this person is concerned about, then he can again go through this thing. . . . Now, this time around does it match or not?

Carl: After they have told him?

After they have given him some details, is there some kind of match . . . a little bit?

Carl: Yeah. It was more of a humorous thing than anything else. (OK.) But he probably would not have known that if he hadn't asked the questions. "How specifically am I a turkey? (laughter) In the past he probably wouldn't have questioned it. He would have just thought, "Yeah, I'm a turkey." Either that, or "Screw you, you're a turkey, too."

Right. Screw you, OK. Now watch him, as he again goes through this procedure of deciding what response to make to this person. You may have done this already. And then in the future is there any way that he wants to behave differently? Is there anything useful? And sometimes, if it is just a playful thing, it may be just kind of banter back and forth and doesn't matter, and there is not really any impetus to change behavior. . . .

OK, now I want you to run through it one more time. This time some real weirdo comes up just out of the blue on the street and makes some weird comment that you can't make head nor tail out of. (OK.) And again he asks, you know, "Well, can you say more about this?" Or, "How specifically?" or something like that. And he just gets "word salad" back, you know; this is a schizophrenic who just got loose from the hospital or something. And when you make a movie of what his pictures are, and what you can remember of what just happened, it just doesn't match at all. (Right.) And at a certain point you say, "Thanks, but no thanks," or "Excuse me," or something like that. You make a concerted effort to find out what the person means, and if there is any real information in this— or is this just an insult that comes out of their own internal space, in which case you can safely dismiss it, because you don't have any— (*Carl:* It's not worth it.) It's not worth it, because it doesn't have information that you want to use to change your behavior in the future, right?

Carl: You are not going to learn from it.

Right. OK, now, watching that Carl over there go through all that, I gather this feels real good. Right? (Real good.) It looks nice? (Looks nice.) Is there *any* problem with any part of that? Is there any part of that that you would want to adjust in any way, or that you have any concerns about? . . .

Carl: The only thing is that I just—I want this to happen. I want to be in there. I don't want to be dissociated! (laughter)

Well, that is the next step. But it looks good out there, right? (No problems.) OK, great.

OK, gradually reach out and beckon to that one out there (Steve demonstrates reaching out with his arms and then bringing them slowly back toward his chest), and very gradually, at your own speed, just bring him in to you, and make him totally a part of you. (Carl reaches out and brings the other Carl back in. As he does this, there are a lot of nonverbal shifts—deeper breathing, color changes, etc.—that indicate a powerful integration with a lot of feeling.) . . .

Take a couple of minutes, to take that all in. . . . Just hang out there for a while. . . . (Carl wipes his eyes.) This is a biggie for you, isn't it? (Carl nods.) I am glad you came up here. That's good. . . . So you just take a little time to hang in there for a while and just let all that stuff kind of settle down. Take as much time as you want. I am going to go through stuff with the group; you just hang out there.

OK, do you have any questions? You can take a look at the outline sheet if you want. OK.

Dee: Well, either I missed it or something, but you didn't have him do one, that I saw, where somebody that he *really* cared about, respected, admired, and he was really close to, said something totally tacky, tasteless, and vicious to him.

When you are in a small group, make sure that they do that with you. (laughter)

Dee: OK. Well, I mean it is fine if some clown walks up to you, you go (she shrugs) "Who cares?" But if somebody you care about does that, it is not all that easy to take.

It is different, right. Now he actually picked somebody in his own family—

Carl: That's what I started out with.

So he actually started out with something like that.

Carl: Because, you know, as far as I am concerned, that is the hardest—was the hardest for me, and I didn't get angry at the person who gave it to me. I was angry at myself for not being able to respond to it in the way I would like to. And, as far as my own family goes, I know that they love me in the first place, and in their eyes it's constructive. It's just that the way I was receiving it, you know. I would automatically second-guess myself on something I was doing, and automatically just go, "Yeah, I'm this rotten person." And so I knew that their intentions were good; it was just how I responded to it. And being able to dissociate and watch me dissociate—

Dee: OK. But would you have felt the same way if what they said— like you said "Oh, yeah, I can see that that's valid." Suppose that it was totally not valid for you. It might have been for them and they might think so, but it is absolutely not real to you that that is true. Would you have felt the same way?

Carl: As I was watching it like that? Yes. I am protected. Before, in the past, it just was coming right into me. (Carl gestures toward his mid-chest.) But to be able to see what they are telling me up on a picture and have that dissociation is just like the fast phobia cure, it enables you to experience something, and be apart from it, so you don't have to associate and feel like crap about it. (Take it in physiologically.) That's right. You could say anything to me right now, if you want, and we can test it out.

Dee: Well, I don't have anything mean to say to you.

I have taught this a lot of times, but you have really been the slowest. (Carl looks up and smiles.) This is testing. This is called testing, right?

Dee: I thought he was the most touching. He got me right in my heart.

If there is a particular situation, Dee, that is the one that always gets you or something like that, I recommend that you don't use that as the *first* thing to run through this. Because when you're first learning to drive, you don't get in a car and go straight to Le Mans or Daytona Beach or something like that—you learn, hopefully, on a dirt track or a football field or something like that. But by all means do use this with whatever is for you the most difficult kind of criticism to take, whether it's a boss or a spouse or a child, or whoever. By all means use it at some point, *after* you have gained some fluency with the different steps, because otherwise you may get stuck in one step and the whole thing may fall apart. By all means test it. And I agree with what I think is the intent of your comment: "Well, you know, this may work on some things, but how about those real tough ones?" By all means do it on the tough ones. It will work on that if you really install the system, because the strategy—just like the fast phobia cure—establishes that dissociation so that you can watch it all out there. One of the lovely things about this installation method is if the you out there screws up—

Carl: You are protected from it.

You are protected. You can just watch it, and then you can just back up the movie and say, "OK" and you make some adjustment, and then you run it forward again, so that—

Carl: You have total control, whatever happens.

Follow-up Interview

So it has been about two weeks now. So, tell the folks out there.

Carl: Well, after the criticism strategy was installed, a couple of people here would—out of the clear blue sky—just walk up to me and call me a jerk and stuff, and then they would start laughing because they were just trying to test it, but—

So that wasn't a very good test, right?

Carl: No, the real world is where it needed to be done. And in my job, I never realized this before, but I go into people's homes, and I remove equipment that my company has installed there. And when I remove it, it leaves holes in their walls, and everywhere. And they originally signed a contract that we are not responsible or anything. I am the person there, and I am the one that they yell and scream at. I never realized before that that would bother me, you know, unconsciously. But when it would happen in the last two weeks, I would automatically take a step back, and I am doing it right now because I am remembering it. And when it would first start happening, it would consciously happen and I would see it, and decide whether it was worth it or not, and go on from there. And the more it would happen, the faster it became. So the people I work with, they just wired it in really great for me. So I was almost reframing. It was like, you know, "Keep it up, man! This is great for me."

The more the better. (Yeah.) That is how it works. When you install a new system like that, the more it gets to run, the more automatic it becomes. Now, you said consciously you'd take a step back. It was that you consciously *noticed*, right? (Right.) It wasn't that you would consciously think about doing it, right?

Carl: No, no, no, no. That happened on its own. A couple of times during driving—I do a lot of driving—I would cut somebody off and it would work real well there, too. (laughter) Especially, you know, in the past I would always be going, "Oh, I am a terrible driver," and then if it was warranted, I'd say, "Yeah, well, next time I have to do a little bit better."

Good. I was a little worried there for a moment that I'd turned you into a lousy driver.

Carl: I think the best test happened yesterday. I got my hair cut, and I felt pretty good about it. I thought it looked pretty good, and I went home, just to my parents. I don't live there, but I just went by to see them. And I said, "I got my hair cut, Mom." And she looked at me and she goes, "What about the back?" back here, because usually I get it all cut. And she was serious, you know, "What about the back?" And instantly: step back, "Is this warranted?" "No." It was really powerful. And for it to be with her—the family scene—and for me not to plan, it was totally unconscious, and it was really powerful. So, I am a success.

OK. Thanks a lot.

Carl: Thank you.

(It is now over eight months later, and Carl still responds well to criticism.)

Review of the Strategy

1. Install the strategy in a dissociated state. *"Ann, see yourself out there in front of you. That Ann is about to learn a new way to respond to criticism."* Do whatever you need to do to maintain the dissociation. *"You can see Ann as far away as you want to, or in black and white, and you can put up a plexiglass barrier in front of you if that helps you stay here as an observer."*

Always use pronouns and location words, such as *"her, out there,"* to keep that distance and dissociation. Be sure to watch for the nonverbals of dissociation. When Carl was first up here, he started seeing himself over there, and then his shoulders and head came back, which was a good indication that he was getting more fully dissociated. So make sure that the client looks different when she is dissociated than when she is associated.

A few people will prefer to use auditory dissociation— hearing themselves on a tape recorder at another location in space—or very rarely even kinesthetic dissociation—feeling themselves with their fingertips at another location in space. You can also use the "as if" frame or vague language for people who don't consciously visualize: "*Pretend* that you can see yourself over there." "Get a sense that you are behind a plexiglass shield."

2. Dissociate from the criticism.   *"That Ann over there is about to be criticized. Watch and listen as she immediately dissociates from the criticism."* There are various ways for her to do this. One way is for that Ann over there to see herself getting criticized. Another way is for her to print the words of the criticism out in space at about arm's length, or she can step out of her body and see herself receiving the criticism. If simple dissociation alone isn't enough to keep that Ann in front of you in a resourceful state, try using some other supporting submodality shifts. Have *that* Ann make that dissociated picture of being criticized smaller, farther away, transparent, dimmer, or any other submodality shift that sufficiently diminishes her response.The dissociation prevents the immediate bad feelings that so many people experience, and it also provides the objective viewpoint necessary for the next step.

3. Make a dissociated representation of the content of the criticism.   *"Watch Ann as she makes makes a movie of what the criticizer is saying."* Again, that Ann can make this representation smaller and farther away in order for her to maintain a resourceful state. Some people make such big, bright, and close pictures of the "awful" thing they did, that it's very difficult for them to maintain a resource state. She can move it far enough away, or whatever, so that she can be comfortable, yet still see it clearly.

Before you can evaluate criticism, you need to *understand* it. What does this person mean? If someone says, "You're twenty minutes late; now we'll either have to rush or be late to the movie," you can easily make a reasonably detailed internal representation of that information in all major representational systems.

However, often criticism is too vague to understand well. If someone says, "You're a skunk," or "You're inconsiderate," that Ann will have to gather more specific information in order to know exactly what the criticizer means. Before asking for more information, it is always useful to pace the criticizer in some way: "I'm concerned that you think I'm a skunk," "I appreciate your honesty in telling me that," "I'm sorry that I upset you," etc. Then you can ask, "What specifically did I do that was inconsiderate?"

"Watch that Ann continue to gather information until she can make a clear and detailed representation of the criticism in all major representational systems."

4. Evaluate the criticism, gathering information when necessary. *"Watch Ann as she compares her representation of the criticism with all other information she has about the situation, in order to find out if they match or mismatch."* The simplest and most direct way to do this is to have Ann rerun her own remembered movies of the event and compare them with a movie of the criticism. She can also run movies of the event from different viewpoints, including that of the criticizer, an onlooker, or another relevant person. If she has comments from other onlookers, these may also be useful in evaluating whether or not the criticism contains valid, useful information.

If there is a complete mismatch between the memory and the criticism when she does this, she may need to back up to Step 2 and gather more information about the criticism. For instance, she may not have understood that when the criticizer said she was "shouting" and "ranting," he meant that the volume and pitch of her voice increased by 10%, and this is something that he is very sensitive to because of a history of being abused.

If there is still a complete mismatch after repeated information-gathering, it may be time for her to conclude that she simply disagrees. The criticizer may be hallucinating or in some other way internally generating experience. His comments aren't really about her, but about himself, his past history, etc. Of course it's also possible that she may have amnesia for what he's talking about, or that her perspective is so different that she hasn't yet found a way to understand the criticizer. Depending on the situation, it may or may not be worthwhile for her to continue to work toward understanding.

Usually there will be at least some match between that Ann's representation and the critizer's. When this is true, she can acknowledge the parts that match, and ask for more information about the parts that she doesn't yet understand.

When the two representations do match, this is equivalent to saying that according to her best information—and the more she has, the better!— the criticism is accurate feedback information that is useful for her to know about.

5. Decide on a response. *"Watch Ann as she decides what she wants to do."* So far her only response to the criticizer has been pacing and information-gathering. It is now time for a response, even if it's only an all-purpose response, such as, "Thank you for bringing this to my attention; I'll have to give this some serious thought." Ann's response will depend on who she is as a person—her outcomes, criteria, values—as well as the context and the criticism itself. She may want to offer an apology, or even some kind of restitution to compensate for what she's done. On the other hand, if her intention was to annoy the criticizer, a simple, "You got my message" may be appropriate. If there is a complete mismatch, she can respond by saying simply, "That's certainly not the way I remember it." If his view is a possible interpretation of her behavior, she can say, "That certainly isn't the message I meant to convey, but I can see how you could understand it that way. What I *intended* to do was Y," and clarify the misunderstanding.

"Observe Ann as she carries out her chosen response."

6. Consider changing future behavior.

"Ask the Ann out there, 'Do you want to use the information you got from this criticism to act differently in the future?' " If so, watch as Ann selects the new behavior(s), and future-paces the new behavior(s).

In step five, you watched Ann respond to the criticizer in the "present." In this step, you watch Ann decide whether she wants to adjust her behavior in order to get a different response from the criticizer or others in the future. If she does want to be different in the future, now is the time for her to select or create new behaviors and future-pace them into the appropriate contexts. If she doesn't have time at the moment, she can take a minute to carefully record what she wants to change, and program herself to make these changes at a specific time and place when she'll have time to do it. This is future-pacing the process of future-pacing to a time when she can do it more thoroughly.

7. Repetition.   It's useful to repeat the strategy two or three times. Each rehearsal should utilize one or more of the major optional elements in the strategy that were not used in previous rehearsals. For instance, if the criticism in the first example was detailed and specific, the next criticism should be so vague that Ann has to gather information in order to make a representation of the criticism. *"Watch Ann over there in another situation where she is about to be criticized. This time the criticism will be very general, so she will have to gather detailed information about what the criticizer means. Watch and listen carefully as Ann goes through the same sequence in this situation."* The major optional elements are:

   a. *Gathering information* when the criticism is vague.

b. *Matching* or *mismatching* when comparing the representation of the criticism with your own representation of the same event.

c. *Deciding on a response* in the immediate situation.

d. *Using the information* in the criticism to select and future-pace new behavior for the future.

Usually about three rehearsals are enough to install the new strategy. When you think the strategy is installed, you can test: "*Ask Ann if she understands this method for responding to criticism well enough to automatically use it any time in the future that you receive criticism.*" If the answer is "No," identify the specific lack of understanding and fix it, or observe her as she runs through the sequence a few more times.

8. Reassociate with the part of you that learned this strategy. It is time to reassociate with the dissociated self in order to incorporate the strategy. "*You have just watched a part of yourself learn a new way of responding to criticism in a useful way. I want you to thank her for being a special resource to you in this way. . . . Now I want you to actually reach out with your hands and arms, embrace that Ann, and gently bring her back into you, taking all the time you need, so that all those learnings will be available to you immediately and unconsciously any time you find yourself being criticized in the future.*"

As with any NLP technique, you want to be sensitive to any possible objections along the way, and adapt what you do accordingly.

Installation

If you think of a criticism made about you, and use that content to go through the steps of the strategy in your imagination, you can install the strategy in yourself by a process of dissociated rehearsal. The strategy can become really smooth and automatic if you repeat this process with several different kinds of criticism from different people in your life, and in different contexts, so that you generalize and use all elements in the strategy. Although you can install this strategy in yourself, since so many people respond so quickly and "phobically" to criticism, we have found it very helpful to have someone else help you establish the dissociation and offer guidance as you install this strategy.

Summary
1. **Install the strategy in a dissociated state.**
2. **Dissociate from the criticism.**
3. **Make a dissociated representation of the content of the criticism.**

4. **Evaluate the criticism, gathering information when necessary.**
5. **Decide on a response.**
6. **Consider changing future behavior.**
7. **Repetition.**
8. **Reassociate with the part of you that learned this strategy.**

Testing

All good NLP work involves testing before and after intervening, to be sure that useful change has occurred. We have presupposed that your client has already demonstrated to you an unuseful response to criticism. Since behavioral testing is always the best, you can test by saying—with congruent nonverbal analogue behavior: "I've taught this process to a lot of people, but you sure asked the *dumbest* questions," and observe his response. It can also be useful to test in the client's imagination with all the major different contexts (people, places, situations, etc.) that previously were problematic, to make sure that he has generalized this new skill fully.

Discussion

Since few people have a good way of evaluating criticism objectively and responding to it congruently, we have found this strategy very useful for most clients. The people to whom we have taught it report that they have easily taught it to others as well, so it is the pattern itself that works; the change is not due to a particular personal style, charisma, or other chance events. Some of our students routinely install it in all their clients because it is so useful. When you teach someone this strategy, you are actually installing a piece of internal reference, a way for people to depend more on their own internal evaluations while remaining open to external feedback. Do you have any questions?

Joan: You used a double dissociation to teach the strategy. And then you bring that part of you in. Now when you get criticized, do you have one or two dissociations?

You just have one dissociation. You have reintegrated the first dissociation that you used to learn the strategy.

Mark: Give some suggestions about how you could have someone generate this strategy into the past. I'm thinking of one particular client who is still smarting from old criticisms.

Here we used a criticism in the present; you can do the same thing in the past. Think of a criticism that really devastated you in the past, and see yourself out there about to get that criticism. When you go through the whole strategy, you will be effectively combining this strategy with the changing personal history pattern. Some people have used this strategy to review difficult past relationships and learn from them. As they gather information, often they have been deeply touched by important things they learn, and have felt a sense of resolution and relief. This kind of information can also have a healing effect on continuing relationships.

Sylvia: I don't have too much trouble with others' criticism, but a lot of the time I criticize myself, and I am more critical of myself than anyone else is. How can I deal with that?

You can use the same strategy with an internal voice, or with whatever part of you criticizes you. Just dissociate from that voice. And let me give you a great way to do it. Where do you hear this voice in your head?

Sylvia: Where do I hear it in my head? What geographical—

Yeah. Do you hear it over here (gesturing right) or here (gesturing left) or here (gesturing top) or right in the middle, or . . . ?

Sylvia: More in the left side of my head.

Can you hear that voice now? Imagine it saying something critical to you. What kind of thing might it say? "You didn't do that very well," or—

Sylvia: Yeah. "What a stupid thing to do."

"What a stupid thing to do." Great. Now, hear that voice come out of your left big toe. . . . (laughter) It is *really* different, isn't it?

Sylvia: Yeah, it sure is.

That provides that distance, that auditory dissociation. And then you can go through the same strategy with that internal critical voice.

Bill: While we are doing this installation, everybody's forewarned that what's about to come is criticism, so the shield can be up in advance. Real life isn't like that; it seems like I feel bad first, and then I realize, "Oh, I just got criticized," but the knife's already in me.

This has never been a problem. If you find that it is a problem for you, then take a little time to determine your "early warning system" for criticism. How do you know that someone is starting to say something about you? Use that as the starting cue for installing the strategy. It is a logical possibility, but it has never been a practical problem in installing this strategy.

Sally: Can you use this strategy in situations where someone else is criticizing you to another person, and it is coming back to you through that third person?

Sure. The input channel doesn't mattter. The same strategy works if someone criticizes you on the telephone, or in writing, or in any other way. The input could also be purely nonverbal. Someone can look "pained," or sigh, or turn away with a "disgusted" look, or whatever. If you want to be absolutely sure, you can use a different input channel for each rehearsal, to force the person to generalize to different modes of input.

Although fewer people complain about it, we have noticed that many people are just as vulnerable to flattery as they are to criticism. People can "butter them up" with compliments and then take advantage of them, or blind them to problem behaviors that need correcting. One of our favorite paradox fortune cookie fortunes says, "You are much too intelligent to be affected by flattery." (laughter) If you don't carefully evaluate compliments, you can easily believe things about yourself that aren't true. People with flattering self-delusions are less open to feedback, and when it finally becomes unavoidable, it's usually much more devastating; people not only have to adjust to the mismatch between their behavior and someone else's criticism, they also have to adjust to the mismatch between their behavior and their own delusions. Sometimes people who don't have a way to evaluate criticism or flattery simply avoid critical people, and surround themselves with people who will only flatter them. While this makes life more pleasant for them in the short run, they miss out on a lot of useful information, and sooner or later they usually bump their noses when "cloud nine" runs into a mountaintop.

This strategy is equally useful for people who would like to evaluate *compliments* before responding to them. All that is needed is a small change in the way the initial cues for step one are described. Instead of saying, "Dissociate from any criticism," you say, "Dissociate from *any* comments about yourself or your behavior, whether complimentary or critical." The only other added change is an explicit instruction to be sure to associate with any complimentary comments you evaluate as true, so that you can fully enjoy them.

One very generative consequence of teaching this process is that people change in the direction of having much more of an internal reference, while at the same time becoming much more open to information from external sources. This is the best of all possible worlds: to be open to all sources of information, yet be able to make your own decisions based on your own values, outcomes, and criteria.

IX

*Accessing Kinesthetic States**

Now we'd like to teach a very easy way to get a deep and powerful access for any kinesthetic resource state. This pattern is particularly effective for accessing drug states. Those of you who have tried recreational drugs know that there are certain undesirable consequences such as the cost, the law, and the fact that you cannot get back to your normal state very easily. Drugs are quite useful for taking you into states, but once you're there it's usually hard to get back. Sometimes you need to drive home or do something else requiring contact with the real world, and the drug state often makes that difficult.

When you can get into a state mentally without drugs, you have the advantage of being able to get back out when you want to, and a lot of the undesirable consequences don't occur. You can easily contextualize your drug state so that it doesn't interfere with the rest of your life. If you teach this process to drug abusers, they can use it to get to the resources that exist in the drug state without all the consequences.

There are also many applications of this technique in medicine and dentistry, especially for pain control. Although medicine is a marvelous science and does a lot of wonderful things, all drugs have side effects. Some have very severe side effects, particularly if you take them in large quantities or for a long time, and some people are hypersensitive or allergic to certain drugs.

---

*We learned this method from Richard Bandler, who credits Ed Reese, president of the Southern Insitute of NLP, for first developing it. We have developed the section on redesigning states.

This process is basically an application of the principle that if you chunk an experience down small enough, it's easy to do anything. Our favorite example of this—because it is so bizarre—is the guy who decided to eat a bicycle for the *Guiness Book of World Records*. He ground up a bicycle into very tiny fragments, and over a period of about three months he actually consumed an entire bicycle. I'm sure you can think of more useful applications of the principle of chunking, but this is certainly a memorable one! (laughter)

When you chunk your experience down small enough, you can change state very easily. One of the most powerful things you can do in NLP is find *transition* states. You've all had marvelous states and you have all had terrible states, at some time or other. The question is, "How do you get from one to the other?" When you are depressed, you can remember being happy but it is hard to get there. Simply knowing that there was a state that is different is often not enough; you need to know *how to get there*. A lot of people build castles in the sky, and NLP's job has been to construct stairways. NLP is a technology that gets you there.

Psychoactive drugs are a very powerful way of getting to another state of consciousness. People who have taken LSD entered very different realities, some of which were useful, some of which were not. But they typically had no way to get there on their own. They usually had no way to make a connection between the learnings they made, or the experiences they had in the drug state, and their regular life. As a result, many became addicted to various drugs, psychologically if not physiologically.

We'd like to mention one other thing before we demonstrate. This method requires that you have some memory of going into the drug state. If you don't have a fairly good memory of what occurred as you entered the drug state, that will make this process a little tougher. However, most people actually have an adequate memory for this, even when they don't initially think so.

Now let's go ahead and demonstrate the process. Is there anybody here who would like to access a drug state? You don't need to say anything about the drug itself.

Elicitation Demonstration

1. Kinesthetic Sequence

Stan, the first step is to discover the kinesthetic feelings that occurred *as this drug started to take effect*. We want you to chunk it down into fairly small pieces, or stages, as you went into that state. For instance, there might have been a little flush somewhere, or a little tingling, or a feeling of relaxation in some part of your body. We want to get the *sequence* of feelings that occurred. For instance, you might have experienced a sudden warm rush that went through your whole body, but if you examine it carefully, it probably started in one place and then spread somewhere else in stages.

Stan: I'm having trouble thinking of which drug I want to use.

Well, just pick any one; once you know how to do it, you can use the same process on the rest of them. It really doesn't matter which one you pick in order to learn the process.

Stan: OK. The initial one that pops into my head is a feeling at the top of my brainstem of warmth, lightness, . . . a real mild, gentle buzz, a vibration.

This is actually a kinesthetic vibration rather than an auditory one, right? If we chunked it down even further, is there any *sequence* to those several things you mentioned? There is warmth; there is the vibration—

Stan: I think actually lightness comes first, . . . and then warmth, and then the vibration.

Are all those sensations in the same spot?

Stan: Yes, basically. . . . Next is a kind of tightness—what I think of as a mask, a bandit's mask around my eyes. . . . (Stan's voice becomes very slow.) Next there is a slight tingle on the inside of the upper lip. . . .

As we are gathering information there is a strong tendency, of course, for him to begin to reaccess that state and "go away." That's why some of you are laughing; you noticed that his eyes are glazing over, and he's starting to tilt off his chair. What's next, Stan? You need to come back here now and then to communicate with us.

Stan: In the solar plexus, . . . it could be excitement, or fear. I'm trying to figure out what physical sensation that is.

"Excitement" and "fear" are *evaluative* labels for the sensation. Describe the sensation itself in terms of warmth, tingling, lightness, heaviness, tightness, or some word that is *descriptive* of the sensation, rather than evaluative.

Stan: Actually, it's a little higher than my solar plexus. It's at my esophagus, kind of like a warmth. It feels red. (He gestures from upper chest to lower chest, along the midline.)

So it starts up near your neck and goes down. Is there anything else? We've got quite a list here already. By this time you're fairly well into that state, right?

Stan: Yeah.

Let's arbitrarily number this into six chunks, just to keep track of it all. Now, we'd like you to rehearse one more time, for two reasons. First, so that you can review it and make it a nice, smooth sequence. Second, we want you to notice if anything has been left out. Is this the proper sequence? 1. Brainstem lightness, 2. Warmth, 3. Vibration, 4. Bandit's mask, tightness around the eyes, 5. Lip tingle, 6. Midline warmth (throat to solar plexus). Now go through that on your own. Would you like me to talk you through it? Would that make it easier?

Stan: I just went through it. I identified them as I went through, in sequence.

Great. Notice how his face is flushed. We're interested in his subjective experience, but that's a nice external confirmation that this sequence is useful for accessing an altered state. Do any of you have questions about how to do this? You need a sequence of specific small-chunk kinesthetic feelings. If he says secondary evaluative words like "anxiety," "fear," or "excitement," you don't want that. You want primary sensations: "warmth," "tingling," "lightness," "heaviness," "spreading," "radiating"— whatever words appropriately describe his kinesthetic sensory experience. Drugs typically work directly on the physiology, so you can always depend on getting a kinesthetic sequence; Your experience is a result of the action of the drug on the nervous system, the endocrine system, and everything else.

2. Other Submodality Shifts

Now that we have a list of the kinesthetic shifts that Stan experiences as he enters the drug state, the next step is to determine what *other* submodalities change along with these kinesthetic shifts.

Stan, go through the stages we have identified, and notice what submodality changes occur in other systems, such as visual and auditory. When you go back to these sensations of lightness, warmth, and vibration in your brainstem, does anything happen to your hearing? Does anything happen to what you see? Either with your eyes open or shut, what other changes in submodalities do you notice?

Stan: My hearing. I was going to say it became more acute; I became more aware of the noise of the air conditioner. Also, as I was going through it, I began to notice more visual acuity—more awareness of smaller details.

Do you focus on one area and delete the rest, like suddenly noticing someone's nose or the color of a pair of pants? Or is it something else? Can you describe it in a little more detail?

Stan: I became more aware of *changes*, of smaller increments. It wasn't like picking out a detail on a still object, but rather becoming more aware of movements or changes.

Is there any sequence between the auditory and the visual shifts? . . . How are they connected with the kinesthetic sequence?

Stan: The auditory shift happened first. It started when I went through the lightness, warmth, vibration. And then I began to notice many smaller visual details.

Is this before you feel the mask? We want to know the sequence. If you have some doubt, you can deliberately try both ways, to find out which feels more congruent. For instance, you could try noticing visual detail and then noticing the mask of tightness around your eyes. Or you could try noticing first the mask and then the visual details. Which feels most comfortable or natural?

Stan: I feel the mask first, and then see the visual details.

So you feel the mask around your eyes, and then see the visual movements and details. Then you feel the inside of your upper lip tingle. What else changes when that occurs?

Stan: That reinforces the lightness, warmth, and vibration in my neck.

OK. So this tingling in your lip reinforces the sensations in your neck that you started with. Sometimes you get repetition like this. Rather than having a sequence of *different* events, you have a repetition of a single one that amplifies the state.

Does anything else change when you feel the warmth move down your midline from esophagus to solar plexus?

Stan: That also strengthens the sensations in my brainstem.

Now, Stan, we'd like you to rehearse what we have so far. Do you want us to talk you through it a little?

Stan: Sure.

First you have the sensation in your brainstem of lightness, then warmth, and then vibration. As you feel those, you can hear little auditory changes. Then you feel the tightness around your eyes, the mask. And then you notice little movement details, whether you have your eyes open or not. And then you feel the tingling inside your upper lip, which reinforces those sensations in your brainstem. Then that midline warmth spreads from your esophagus to your solar plexus, which also reinforces those feelings in your brainstem. . . .

As you go through this, do you have a sensation of entering that particular drug state?

Stan: It's not quite as powerful as the actual drug state has been at times, but it's as powerful as it has been at other times.

Are we missing anything? You just had an opportunity to go through it a couple of times; is there anything else?

Stan: No, I covered all the bases.

Now any time you want to reaccess this state, this process gives you a very specific piecemeal way of doing it, a kind of recipe that makes it relatively easy. You had no trouble doing it here, even when you were exploring it for the first time. Each time you do it, it will be even easier, and usually it will also become faster. After you do it a few times, probably all you'll have to do is start feeling those feelings in your brainstem, and then the rest of the sequence will happen automatically.

Redesign Demonstration

3. Adjusting Submodalities

The next step is redesign. How can you make the state even better? You've probably heard about chemists and "designer drugs." You can also make designer drug *states* by altering submodalities in the sequence, or by adding others. You simply experiment to find out what changes the state in ways that you like. Stan, we want you to try a few things and then report back. What happens if those sensations in your brainstem spread farther up and down your neck? . . .

Stan: That increases the state a little.

Now try changing the sensation of tightness around your eyes to tingling. . . .

Stan: That reduces the state.

OK. Try adding sparkle to each of the small changes you notice visually. . . .

Stan: That increases it a lot.

So you can experiment in this way to find out how to modify the state. There are so many things you can try. What if you make those sensations thicker? What if those sensations changed from warm to cool, or spread from the brainstem up over your skull? You can have a lightness like a bubble with a very sharply defined edge, or one that is diffuse, as if it were made of fur. You can have lots of little bubbles of lightness instead of one big one, and so on.

Stan, are there any aspects of this drug state that are unpleasant to you?

Stan: There is a heaviness or lethargy that I'd like to change sometimes; at other times it's OK.

Good. Now experiment to discover how you could lighten that heaviness while maintaining the rest of the state. For instance, feel that heaviness now . . . and then imagine that your whole body has little bright sparkles all over its surface. . . .

Stan: That does lighten the heaviness considerably.

A lucky guess. You found earlier that sparkles intensified the state, and bright sparkles are more likely to get you "up" than "down." Of course, there are many other things you could try, and some may work even better.

4. Adjusting the Sequence

So far we have changed or added submodalities, but we have left the sequence as it was. You can also change the *sequence* of your experiences to alter the state. For instance, Stan, what would happen if the tingling inside your upper lip happened right after the brainstem sensation? . . .

Stan: That does seem a little stronger; that whole set of sensations in my brainstem, the high sensation in my head, is different. It takes the intensity up a notch. When I did it, the vibrations were lifting, rising.

It certainly looks different. What if you felt the mask of tightness around your eyes *first,* and then went to feelings in your brainstem? . . .

Stan: That one doesn't help.

That decreases his response, and you can verify this externally by observing his nonverbal behavior. He doesn't go as far into the state with that shift. What if you felt warmth first, then lightness, and then vibration? . . .

Stan: Vibration first works best.

OK, try vibration first. . . . That looks really good! Some of the things you try will increase the state, and some of them will decrease it. Again, these are just a few examples of how you can resequence the experience in order to change it.

5. Compressing the Sequence

One thing that often happens when you resequence steps is that the whole process tends to happen *faster*. When it's compressed into a shorter time period, the intensity often increases. You can also simply run the original sequence faster to increase the intensity. As we have Stan go through it repeatedly, he will tend to do that automatically. The actual drug may take ten or fifteen minutes to take effect, but once we have the sequence, Stan can run through it all in a few seconds. After he does this a few times, it will streamline and become unconscious. Pretty soon all he'll have to do is access the first sensation, and the rest of the sequence will happen automatically; it will be like riding a wave.

Stan, do you have any specific questions? You can probably think of times when you would want to access this state. Do you have any questions about how to do it?

Stan: No. I think you showed me how.

OK. Thanks very much. Let me review the steps in this process:

Outline: Accessing a Kinesthetic State

A. Elicitation
1. Access the sequence of small-chunk kinesthetic experiences.
2. Determine which visual and auditory submodality shifts occur at each stage of the kinesthetic sequence.

B. Redesign
3. Adjust, add or subtract submodalities in the sequence.
4. Change the order of the sequence.
5. Compress the sequence, so it runs faster.

The Brain is a Coincidence Detector

As far as we know, this technique works in the following way. The brain is a coincidence detector. Billions of rat-, dog-, and psychologist-hours have gone into determining that contiguity in space and time is the most significant determinant of learning. Your brain will learn any sequence of events that happens close in space and time.

How many of you have seen the movie *All of Me*? In it there is a guru from the Himalayas who has never seen a flush toilet. As he pushes the handle, the water gurgles and the phone happens to ring. He flushes the toilet again and the phone rings again. His timing happens to be perfect; each time he flushes the toilet, the phone rings, and he keeps doing it. Finally, of course, the phone stops ringing, and he looks at the toilet as if it's broken! That's a silly example, but it's what we do whenever we connect two external events that happen close together in time.

In one of Skinner's operant conditioning experiments with pigeons, he dropped a food pellet into the cage every few seconds, no matter what the pigeon did. Whatever behavior the bird happened to be doing at the time got reinforced. So if it was standing on one leg, or raising a wing, it would tend to repeat that behavior. Ten seconds later when the pellet came down again, that behavior was reinforced even more. He got some pretty bizarrely "superstitious" pigeons, because the pigeon's brain, like our brain, is a coincidence detector—in this case connecting an external event to an internal behavioral response.

Recently it has been discovered that the brain can even condition the immune response. Experimenters conditioned the immune response in mice to an odor. The mice had a tube implanted through which the experimenter could give them a little shot of bacteria that would challenge the immune system; at the same time they presented an odor. The immune system would respond and overwhelm the bacteria. They did this five or six times, using blood assays to find out how the immune system was responding. Then they presented the odor alone, and the immune system responded in the same way as when it was challenged by bacteria! That single experiment has enormous ramifications for all the diseases in which the immune system is known to be depressed or overactive—allergies, cancer, autoimmune diseases like rheumatoid arthritis, etc.

Another confirmation of this is that allergies can often be cured by accessing and anchoring a resource state in which the person doesn't respond to the allergen. A lot of the coincidences that your brain notices and responds to are completely unconscious. They are the kind of responses that Milton Erickson often called "the things you know, but you don't know that you know."

Drugs and Anchors

Since your brain is a coincidence detector, it notices that every time you take a particular drug, you get a certain set of kinesthetic sensations. Those particular sensations, in that particular sequence, occur *only* when you have that physiological response to the drug. Since drugs directly affect your physiology, they are anchors that work every time. One of the reasons that drugs are so popular is that they are dependable. No matter what else is happening, or going on around you, when you take that drug, it takes effect.

Of course, that's an overgeneralization, because your physiology will respond differently at different times. If you take a sedative after drinking fifty cups of coffee, you'll get a different response than if you take it after you've had a long hard day and you haven't used any stimulants. If someone goes into an operating room in a very anxious state, there's so much adrenalin and other chemicals in his bloodstream already that the anesthetist will have to use much heavier doses of drugs to put him to sleep—which can increase the likelihood of harmful side effects.

We know several anesthetists who take the time to talk to patients the day *before* the operation. They set up anchors for relaxation and reassurance, and then use these anchors the following day on the way to the operating room. When they do this, they often only need to use about half the usual dosage of anesthetics.

There are also many individual differences in response to drugs. A friend of ours takes much *longer* to respond to drugs, but when she does respond, she responds more *intensely*. She once warned a doctor about this: "Don't give me a second shot just because I don't go out in a specified time." But when she didn't lose consciousness in the normal time, he gave her a second shot anyway. Forty-eight hours later, she came back, luckily.

Despite these differences in response, drugs are very powerful anchors for states. The drug takes you to a certain state. As it takes you there, you have these various experiences that are cues indicating the physiological shifts. By recreating the cues, you can recreate the state shift without the drug.

By changing or resequencing the cues, you can intensify that state or tone it down. Maybe you want to get high but not *that* high. Sometimes people are totally "gone" when they take a drug— they get really loud and wild. Stan's state was quieter, much more internal.

When you want to, you can also change the character of the drug state. Maybe you took a drug and it sent you away internally. Perhaps you had very interesting pictures inside, but you would like to be a little more external from time to time so that you can interact with others. By experimentation, you can find the submodality shifts that will give you that effect.

Chunking

This process chunks down what people have been doing for years in NLP: accessing resource states. "When were you in that excellent state? Where were you? What room were you in?" and so on. This process gets much smaller chunks, which makes the process much easier and more powerful. You've all been in situations when you realize, "Uh, I'm in a bad state. How do I get back to a good one? Well, I kind of remember it, but where is it and how do I get there?" Sometimes it's hard to reaccess it; this process gives you a "yellow brick road" that will take you right there.

Man: How many chunks should there be in the sequence?

We try for around five chunks. *The only point in chunking it down is to make it easy to do.* Sensations often start in one spot and spread throughout the body. Is that one chunk, or two, or twenty? If you think in terms of a set number of chunks, you might get five pieces at the very beginning and only have a small portion of the whole process. Keep your outcome in mind: *to identify how you make the complete transition into the drug state in small-enough chunks that it's easy for you to access that state fully.* Chunking down more than that is a waste of time.

Getting Back Out

Woman: Do people ever have difficulty getting *out* of a self-induced drug state?

Years ago, you heard a lot about LSD "flashbacks," in which people accidentally accessed a previous drug state and then couldn't get back out. More recently, you hear about "Vietnam flashbacks" which are similar. When you methodically teach someone how to enter a state, that's very different from accidentally falling into a state without any sense of control. Since the person doesn't actually have a drug in his bloodstream, as far as I know you can always break his state, even if you have to be outrageous, yell "fire!" or something like that. One of our students works with alcoholics and drug abusers; he has sometimes had to walk them around outside on a cold winter day, wearing only a shirt, to sober them up, but he has always gotten them back out.

If you were working with someone who has a fairly loose grasp on reality you could always play it safe by first discovering her sequence of experience as she *leaves* the drug state, making sure that you have an effective sequence for that before finding out how she enters the drug state. You could also take the sequence that occurs as she enters the drug state and run it *backwards* to bring her out.

If you're concerned about your own safety, there is another thing you might consider doing. Before you induce a drug state on your own, set up a part of you to be a "watchdog" to alert you and bring you out of the drug state if something dangerous or unexpected happens. You can do this with reframing: close your eyes, go inside, and say internally, "I am about to access a drug state. I'm doing it here in what I consider to be a safe environment. I would like some part or parts of me to remain alert to any danger that might occur, or any situation that could have possibilities of unpleasant consequences. The moment there is even a suggestion of danger or harm, please bring me right back out so that I can deal with it in my normal non-drug state, with all my resources available to me. Is there some part or parts that are willing to perform that function for me?" When you receive a confirming unconscious signal, you can feel safe in entering the drug state, knowing that you are protected. Most people already have protective parts that will function in this way, but this is a way to be explicit.

Medical Uses

A majority of drugs are used for pain control and symptomatic relief, and this process has many direct practical applications in this area. Steve uses this when he gets his teeth cleaned, and for many fillings, too. He used to get very tense in the dentist's chair: his stomach would knot up for about six hours afterwards, and for the rest of the day he was pretty wiped out. Now he almost looks forward to going to the dentist, so he can "zone out" and relax.

A friend of ours, Bobbi, was quite ill recently with a kidney infection. She was prescribed antibiotics for the infection and pain-killers for symptomatic relief: Tylenol III, Tylenol IV, or 1,000 mg. of Darvoset. She was supposed to take four of these a day for a month or so. One of them knocks you out for six or eight hours. She had learned the drug state access, but she hadn't had this particular drug before, so she took one of these pills, sat down with a tape recorder, and described all the changes that occurred as she entered the state. She later played it back several times until she knew exactly what went on when she actually took the drug. That gave her exquisitely detailed information for entering that state voluntarily. Bobbi was able to control the pain almost completely with the drug state access. Instead of four pills a day, she took about two a week. The few times she did use the pills were always late in the evening, when she was very tired and didn't feel as if she had the concentration to use the drug state access. If this method were more widely-known, doctors could prescribe far fewer pills—enough for a "learning" dose, and a few extra for extreme circumstances.

When you use this process to access drug states for pain control or other symptomatic relief, you usually want to stay with the sequence you get from that drug, because it was selected to do a particular thing for your body. Hopefully the doctor is right; sometimes she is not.

Assuming the doctor has chosen an appropriate drug, there are two useful ways to experiment. One is to intensify the desired effect of the drug; the other is to eliminate side-effects, such as nausea or drowsiness.

For example, Bobbi had some nausea with Tylenol III, so she noticed what happened in the sequence just before and after she started to feel nauseous. Then she just skipped that step, and noticed a shift in her breathing. There was only one step that created the nausea, and it wasn't essential to the analgesic effect.

Nausea is a response to some experience; if there is no external real-world experience producing it, it's probably a response to an inner experience. Think of all the real-world experiences that produce nausea for you. If you create any of those experiences internally, they can also produce nausea. Often a person's internal pictures start tilting or spinning or sliding around. If you change that, the person won't experience nausea.

We want to warn you to be *much* more cautious about attempting to use this method as a substitute for other drugs—such as antibiotics—whose effects are directed specifically against bacteria, and have minimal physiological or perceptual effects. However, if you can condition the immune response with an odor, who knows what is possible? If I were far from medical help, or had an allergy to the drug, I'd certainly give this process a try.

This method works well for any drug used for symptomatic relief *and* which has distinct perceptual effects. If a drug has minimal perceptual effects, it will obviously be much harder to use perceptual cues to access the state.

Kinesthetic Lead
Woman: You've emphasized starting with the kinesthetic system. With certain psychedelics, the first shift I notice is visual. Can I start with that?

The overall goal is to be able to create this experience for yourself without using the drug. Although the kinesthetic system seems to be particularly powerful, you could start with the visual or auditory systems and then go back to get the accompanying kinesthetic shifts. There are several reasons for starting with the kinesthetic system. It insures that the person is associated, rather than dissociated; if you start with visual or auditory, it's possible that you will be dissociated when you recall the state. Using a kinesthetic lead is also unusual, so it is likely to be subjectively impressive and powerful. We have used the kinesthetic lead a lot for this, and we know it's effective; we haven't experimented much with accessing visual or auditory shifts first.

Individual Differences
Man: Are these sequences specific to individuals, or are there some commonalities in the experiences that different people have with a particular drug?

That seems to depend a lot on the drug. We have seen very wide differences in response to the same psychedelic drug. There is more commonality for drugs that have specific impacts on the physiology: depressants, stimulants, etc. Even then, there is quite a variety of response.

Recreational Uses

After you've elicited your sequence for a particular drug, you can teach it to others, and have them teach you theirs. You can use each other's sequence as a "prescription" to enter that state. It's a great way to start a party; no one has to buy any stuff, or worry about the law, or have trouble driving home later. What has been called a "contact high" is an example of this. If you pace someone else really well, you will also experience the same submodalities that they do.

Once when Steve was in college, most of the people around him were drunk at a party. He hadn't had anything, but he was having fun, too. Another student came up close to him and stared in his face with a puzzled look and said, "You haven't had anything to drink and you're having as much fun as I am. How can you do that?" The student was very puzzled, because he couldn't enter that state without drugs.

Drug Abuse

Human beings have been using and searching for drugs for thousands of years. Drugs do have value, but often they also have serious side-effects. Personally, we are essentially non-druggies. We have each tried a few now and then, but we don't like the disorganization that we usually felt for days afterwards. Drugs hold very little allure for us. For other people, of course, drugs are so alluring that the rest of their lives goes to pieces. But drugs do have useful functions: to relax, have fun, forget troubles, etc. Everything is valuable somewhere; using this process is a way that you can have the benefits of drugs without the problems.

If you work with substance abusers, you can say, "How would you like to be able to get into that state any time you want to, without the expense and difficulty of obtaining the drug, without the problems associated with not being able to get out of that state if you need to, without the legal complications, and without the health problems?" They'll usually say, "Hey, sure. Why not? I can disconnect my pusher." This paces their reality completely, and it's also a solution that the rest of society won't object to. You can then use the drug state access to give them voluntary control over their states. As you do this, you can use other NLP methods to help them integrate and reorganize their personal resources so that they have less need for the drug state (as described in *Reframing*, Chapter 6).

Other Kinesthetic States

We have discussed drug states at length because you can usually depend on getting a robust kinesthetic sequence. In addition, the drug state access technique has useful applications in medicine, especially with respect to the side-effects that certain drugs have. Finally, this pattern has many implications for dealing with the widespread problems resulting from drug abuse.

However, the same process can also be used to access *any* resource state that has strong kinesthetic components. For example, there are many applications for people who want to increase their sexual responsiveness. One seminar participant who was typically very visual accessed a relaxing drug state. When she started experimenting with changing the state, she spontaneously started experiencing strong orgasms, one after the other. You can go after this more directly by accessing a particularly satisfying sexual experience, and then learning how to reaccess this state when you're "not in the mood," but would like to be.

You can also use this process to elicit an unpleasant response, and then redesign the sequence so as to alter the response in a useful way. For example, one man frequently got angry. His sequence for this angry state included a pressure that shifted and intensified as it moved and spread from jaw to stomach to forehead, and then to his whole body. With each step of the sequence he got warmer. When we had him become *cooler* as the sequence progressed, his anger diminished considerably. At the end of the sequence he had a sense of pressure on the inside of his skin, as if his skin was like a balloon being overinflated, until it "popped" into overt anger. By thinking of his skin as permeable, as if it had thousands of tiny holes to let the pressure leak out, he could decrease this state even further. When he decreased his state in this way, he found he felt much more in control and had more choices available for dealing with the problem that caused his angry state.

The Kinesthetic Wave

The same idea that the skin is impermeable can be used to amplify a pleasant kinesthetic state. First think of a pleasant state you have experienced, . . . and then notice the kinesthetic feeling in some detail. . . . Now imagine that those feelings are like a wave that spreads quickly through your body and bounces back with increased intensity whenever it reaches the surface of your skin, continuing to reverberate and intensify throughout your body. . . .

Another seminar participant had been horseback riding as a young woman with a group of handsome young men. Her horse stumbled, and she was thrown. She landed on her back, and was knocked unconscious. When she regained consciousness, all the young men were kneeling around her head talking to her, very concerned and attentive. She was in "seventh heaven," and burst out laughing. When she reaccessed this state, her peals of joyous laughter filled the room. By experimenting, she found that she could control the intensity of the state by touching her outstretched hands to the floor. If she lifted her hands completely off the floor she could go fully into the state, knowing that if it got too intense she could "come down" simply by touching a finger to the floor. Previously she had never let herself go fully into that state, because she was afraid it might take over and she'd lose control. The more you can discover how to control your own system, the less dependent you will be on drugs, other people, or events to get you into pleasureable and useful states.

X

Other Submodality Interventions

There are a number of submodality interventions that are so specific and powerful in their impact that when you come across one, you think to yourself, "I'm going to remember *that*!" Richard Bandler calls these "Briefest Therapy" interventions. Here are some that we have repeatedly found to be very useful.

Mapping Across

In Richard Bandler's *Using Your Brain—for a CHANGE*, there are a number of examples of determining the submodality differences between a problem state and a resource state, and then "mapping across" to transform the problem state into the resource state. The most detailed example of this is in Chapter 6, transforming the structure of confusion into understanding. This is also the method we have used in this book to adjust timelines, create compelling futures, build compulsions, and to shift criteria and reference systems. Although this is one of the simplest submodality methods, the applications seem endless— both for helping individuals change, and for modeling the structure of excellence.

For example, a practitioner from one of our trainings runs a program for delinqents. He taught a girl who hated her parents how to take a representation of them and map across to the submodalities of a friend she liked. After that she could deal with her parents in a friendly way.

You can map across in this way from any problem state to an appropriate resource state—from lethargy to motivation or excitement, from boredom to fascination, from serious to ludicrous, from being stuck to something that used to matter but doesn't matter to you now.

179

One man who was allergic to red wine and dark beer cured himself by taking his representations of them and mapping across to the submodalities of white wine and light beer, which he wasn't allergic to. In some people with multiple personality disorder, it has been reported that one personality can be allergic to a substance, but another personality in the same body isn't. This suggests that submodalities may play a part in how the different personalities keep themselves sorted and separate, and that this information could also be used to integrate them.

Mapping across is also a major element in a new one-session pattern we have developed for people who are grieving over a loss. In a forthcoming book, tentatively titled *From Grief to Gratitude*, we will teach how to replace the emptiness of grief with a sense of fullness, and replace preoccupation with past losses with interest in a satisfying future.

Literal Reframing

The word "reframing" is a visual word, yet many people think of it as an auditory process, "rewording." Although you use words to do reframing, the usual effect is to visually place the problem event into a different frame or background. This can be done metaphorically, but it can also be done very simply and literally.

1. Think of a situation that makes you feel bad when you think of it. This could be an old memory, a current problem situation or limitation, or whatever. . . .

2. Take a good look at the visual portion of that problem experience, . . . and then step back out of it, so that you see yourself in that situation. If you don't visualize in consciousness, just have a "sense" of doing these visual changes, or pretend to do it.

3. Now put a large baroque gold frame, about six inches wide, around that picture, and notice how this changes your experience of that situation. . . .

For most people this will anchor a lighter and more humorous set of feelings that is much more useful for going on to develop new choices in that problem situation.

There are also many other alternative literal frames you can use. You could use an oval frame such as were used years ago for old family portraits, mirrors, and religious pictures. A hard-edged stainless steel frame, a natural or weathered wood frame, or a colored plastic frame might be more useful for someone who doesn't respond to the baroque gold one.

You can also add a number of embellishments after a frame is selected. A shielded museum light mounted over the picture "puts a different light on the subject" than does a votive candle on a stand below it. Actually seeing the framed picture on a museum wall among other pictures, or in someone else's home or office, can add a "different perspective."

You can even go on to pick a favorite—or least favorite— artist and transform your picture into a work done in the style of that artist. What happens if you see it as a Rembrandt, or a Monet?

Fall Down Laughing

1. Think of some situation, or imagine it vividly if you've never actually experienced it, in which you were talking to a friend—preferably someone whom you trust—who has a wealth of wisdom and experience. At some point he (or she) found what you said *so* funny that he "fell down laughing;" he was laughing so hard he had difficulty breathing, and he had to wipe the tears from his eyes as the laughter kept rolling out in spite of his trying to stop it. . . .

2. Now think of some problem or limitation you are experiencing in your life. . . .

3. Now vividly imagine that you tell your friend about this problem you are experiencing. As soon as you have told him the basics of your problem, he "falls down laughing" and can't stop, no matter what you do. . . .

4. Think of your problem again; do you feel differently about it now? About half of the people you do this with will never be able to take that problem quite so seriously again, particularly if the friend who falls down laughing is someone with wisdom and deep understanding. They may still want to change the problem situation, but they will feel much more resourceful and capable of doing it.

Humor and laughter are two of the greatest and least utilized resources that we have available to us. Getting serious about something usually means that you have become so immersed (associated) in a situation that you're stuck with only one way of perceiving it. Humor is a way to break out of that trap by dissociating, taking a deep breath, and looking at things differently.

The other half of the people you do this with will typically get quite angry at being misunderstood or "not taken seriously." Even this *can* be a step in the right direction, because anger is usually a more active and resourceful state than being stuck in helpless feelings of sadness and inadequacy. Anger can be a positive force that gets someone to express her needs and take a stand for something that's important to her. Mere "cathar-sis" is seldom useful, *unless* it is utilized to help someone go on to feel powerful, to identify her outcomes, and then to develop more effective ways of getting them. We make a clear distinction between anger, which can sometimes strengthen and empower a person, and violence, which is typically an indication of lack of choice and impotence.

The Godiva Chocolate Pattern

Richard Bandler developed this pattern to create motivation. You may have noticed that other people are motivated to do a wide variety of things that seem amazing or ridiculous to you. This is because most people get motivated to do things in a fairly random and unsystematic way, one that doesn't necessarily have anything to do with the intrinsic value or benefits of the activity.

One very useful application of this pattern is to change your feelings about tasks that you have *congruently* decided you want/need to accomplish, but don't presently enjoy doing. If you've congruently decided it's important to do, you may as well enjoy it! *Be very careful of ecology with this pattern; you don't want to casually install an intense desire to do something.*

Outline

1. Motivation picture.   Get an *associated* picture of some thing or activity you're wildly compelled to enjoy (chocolate, for instance). Set this aside briefly.

2. Task picture.   Get a *dissociated* picture of yourself doing something you have *congruently* decided you need/want to do, so you might as well enjoy it.

3. Ecology check.   Is there any part of you that objects to your *enjoying* doing the task that you have decided you need to do?

4. Iris pattern.

    a. See the task picture (#2) in your mind, with the motivation picture (#1) right *behind* it. Quickly open up a small hole in the center of picture #2, so that you can see picture #1 through this hole. Make the hole rapidly open as big as you need to in order to get a full feeling response to picture #1.

    b. Now shrink the hole down fast, but *only* as fast as you can maintain the feeling response to picture #1.

    c. Repeat steps 4a and 4b several more times, as fast as you can. The outcome is to connect the feelings of the motivation picture to the task picture.

5. Test.   Look at the task picture #2. Are you drawn to it? If not, repeat step four, or go back to previous steps to be sure you have the right elements.

Besides the obvious therapeutic applications, this pattern also has many business applications with employees who have useful jobs that aren't inherently enjoyable. It can also be used with sales people who have "telephonitis" or "doorknobitis," to make them eager to do "cold calls."

Disruption

It is often very useful to simply ruin an internal representation that gets in someone's way. Someone keeps thinking of a horror movie, or a picture in a newpaper, and it serves no useful purpose that you can determine.

Before using this method, do a very careful ecology check. Disruption creates amnesia. The picture may be useful to the client in some way; it may have information about what to do or what to avoid in the future. If this is so, then it's very important to first extract the useful information and put it in a new picture before destroying the old one, or to use some other intervention that doesn't create amnesia.

Crazing is what happens to tempered glass—like that in a rear or side window in a car—when it shatters. It breaks into thousands of tiny granules and falls apart. Imagine that the visual image you want to get rid of is like a car window, or painted on one. Hit it really hard with a hammer and watch it shatter into thousands of tiny granules and fall apart. You may have to repeat this several times to make it complete and permanent.

A woman called late one evening, extremely distraught and barely coherent. I managed to find out that she had just watched a vivid horror movie in which the main characters killed their parents. The movie was "haunting" her and upsetting her greatly. Since these feelings were installed by a movie, I saw no useful information value in her rerunning the movie and being in a bad state. After she disrupted the movie, her voice immediately became calm, and I took a little time to find out if there was anything in her own life that she needed to deal with.

Another woman was haunted by an image of Michael Jackson. After one hammer blow, only the white glove remained. Two more hammer blows got rid of the glove. Some people report that the image doesn't vanish entirely, but that one or more submodalities shift so that it doesn't bother them any more; the image may become smaller, farther away, or black and white.

You can also tell someone to watch a movie "inside out." We don't know what that means, but people will do interesting and useful things in their heads in response to that instruction. One way to think about "inside out" is that everything at the center of the original movie moves to the outside edge, and everything at the edges becomes compressed into the center.

Another reference experience for disruption is watching a movie where the film stops, and the projection lamp burns a hole in each frame. You can also simply burn an image to ashes.

Other useful reference experiences for disrupting a picture are turning a kaleidoscope, watching a watercolor painting on a sidewalk in the rain, seeing an image in a mirror that shatters, seeing an image in a pond that is disturbed, etc.

You can also use this process in reverse. A woman called me who was very upset because she felt fragmented, "as if I'm juggling too many things to keep track of." Visually, she had many fleeting, moving images. I asked her to imagine that she was seeing all this on the surface of a pond that had been disturbed by a windstorm, and that as the wind died down and the surface gradually smoothed, the fragmented images would gradually begin to coalesce and come back together into a single organized picture. Within a few minutes the picture came back together; she was calm and relaxed, and knew what to do next.

Separating Self from Context

As discussed in Chapter II, many people are troubled by unpleasant feelings in response to other people or events. Often it's useful to disrupt these unpleasant cause-effects, to make room for more enjoyable ones. Here's one way to do that:

1. Think of an unpleasant memory, and run a short movie of it. Notice how you respond to that memory now. . . .

2. See yourself in the picture, dissociated. Use whatever submodality distinctions you can easily use to distinguish between yourself and the context, such as size, color, distance, transparency, etc. For example, if the picture is in black and white, see yourself in color. If the picture is distant, see yourself close.

3. Run the movie forward with *your dissociated self moving at double speed* and *the context moving at half speed* (*not* the reverse!). You will see yourself arrive at the end of the movie before the context does, so he will have to wait there until the context catches up with him. . . .

4. Run the movie *backward* with *yourself at half speed and the context at double speed* (*not* the reverse!). This time the context will arrive at the end of the movie before you do. . . .

5. Now run the movie the way you usually do, to find out if there is a change in your feelings.

6. If there is no change, do it again, this time *associated*, and use size to make yourself bigger than the context.

People usually report a sensation of "scrambled brains" after doing this. This pattern is *very* useful for disrupting anchored cause-effects between context and self. When you go at double speed, the cues occur *after* your responses to those cues. This method uses tempo to disrupt the cause-effect sequence. When the effect happens before the cause, it suddenly doesn't make sense anymore. You can use this pattern in couple or family therapy to "clear the slate" of old unpleasant cause-effects, so that you can install some that are more fun.

Separating Internal State from External Behavior
Sometimes the anchored cause-effects that need to be disrupted are between your *own* behavior and your internal state, rather than someone *else's* behavior and your internal state. This is particularly likely, for example, if you can depress yourself in a context where not much else is happening around you to depress you. Steve Lankton had an elderly client who was stroking her thigh with her hand, muttering, "The pain, the pain." When Steve lifted her hand off her thigh, her hand continued to stroke the air but lost contact with her thigh. She looked startled and said, "The pain is gone!"

Use any submodality to make a distinction between your own external behavior and your internal state. Do this in whatever way seems most appropriate to you. Then run the movie forward, associated, with your internal state at double-speed and your external behavior at half-speed. Then run the movie backward, with your internal state at half-speed and your external behavior at double-speed.

Separating Internal State from Internal Computations (Thinking)
If you get into a bad state by your own thinking, without much help from outside, you can use the same procedure to disrupt those cause-effects. This time, use any submodality to make a distinction between your *thinking* and your internal state. Then run the movie forward with your internal state at double-speed and your computations at half-speed. Then run the movie backward with your internal state at half-speed and your computations at double-speed. Try this both associated and dissociated to find out which works best for you.

Modeling Excellence
The best source for new submodality patterns is modeling people who do something well, to find out how they do it. We usually have our advanced

training groups find skills they can model from each other, and we enjoy doing this ourselves whenever we have the opportunity.

Recently we were driving on a winding road through the Colorado Rockies to our summer residential training. We were planning our presentation, and with the combination of mental concentration and winding roads, I (Connirae) was beginning to feel nauseous. Steve commented, "Well, just become me. I feel fine." Steve was just kidding, but I thought it sounded like a good idea. So I pretended that I was Steve: I took on his voice tone and tempo, posture, muscle tone, etc. The moment I did this, my nausea vanished, and I felt fine.

Then we became curious about what made the difference. What internal shifts did I make when I "became Steve" so that my nausea went away? Initially this information was out of consciousness for me. As I thought about it, I gradually noticed that as "Steve," I had acquired a panoramic awareness of the horizon around me; my focus of attention was on the distant circle of mountains touching the sky. It was almost as if that distant circle was my skin—my own boundary. Even when we drove in a narrow valley where I couldn't see very far, internally I had that stable panoramic distant circle of mountains in place all around me. With this in my mind, the movement of the car I was in seemed negligible in comparison. I was primarily responding to the *stability* of the vast external environment, rather than the relatively insignificant movement of the car.

Previously I had been told to look at a distant point to avoid nausea when driving. I had tried that, and it hadn't worked. What made the difference for me was having the entire stable panorama of the surroundings, rather than just looking at one point. Since that time, if we go driving on winding roads, I first carefully notice the geographic panorama around me, and set this in place to maintain my state. I haven't been carsick since.

This was fascinating to us. It fit with what we had previously discovered about each other's internal experience, and helped us understand each other further. Steve *always* has this panorama of his environment in his head— not just when driving in the mountains. It has always mattered to him where we live. Since we spend most of the time working indoors in our office, I've often asked him, "What difference does it make whether we're in a city, or out in the mountains?" Now it makes sense to me that since he always has this panorama around him, it *does* make a difference to him. It's also harder for him to concentrate on a task when the surroundings are chaotic. I can usually concentrate more easily, no matter what kind of environment I'm in. In an ongoing way, I'm more aware of the people who are around. Although I appreciate geographical beauty, I'm pretty flexible about where I live.

In this case rather than asking him questions about submodalities, I identified with Steve by pacing his external behavior. Since external behavior is a manifestation of internal submodalities, if you pace someone very closely, you will also take on his submodalities.

This process of "walking in someone else's shoes" has also been called "deep trance identification," and "switch referential index." In order to make the learnings from this process easily available in the future, and to other people as well, it's essential to go on to identify the specific internal submodalities that characterize the state.

In some ways this particular application may seem trivial. However, the method is the doorway to many other fascinating discoveries about people's skills and abilities. By identifying with someone else who has a skill, and coding what you learn in submodalities, you can understand their "natural" skill and easily teach it to others.

We learned the process of deep trance identification many years ago. Although we found it personally useful, we couldn't specify the essential structure of what we learned by using it. Learning precise submodality distinctions makes it possible to carefully specify the state that you achieve when you identify with someone else. We have enjoyed watching people in the park, or in the mall, or celebrities on TV, taking on their body posture, movement style, voice tone, etc., and noticing how our internal submodalities shift. It's a good way to begin to understand in detail how other people's states are very different from your own. When you identify with your clients, you can get valuable and detailed information about the kind of world they live in. Since there's always the danger that you might be hallucinating, we suggest that you treat the information you get as a *hypothesis* to be tested, rather than truth. Does it allow you to work more effectively with your client? Does it enable you to succeed at a skill which previously *had* been beyond your grasp?

Submodality modeling is an immensely powerful and useful process. Although there is a lot we can do with existing technology, there are still things we can't yet do. We haven't begun to explore the limits of present methods, and newer developments and discoveries will make them even more effective. When you have thoroughly mastered the patterns in this book, we invite you to go on to model other skills and abilities.

"Toto, I don't think we're in Kansas anymore."
—*Dorothy*

Appendix I

Andreas NLP Training Videotapes

These videotapes provide live demonstrations of NLP Submodalities patterns conducted by Connirae and/or Steve Andreas; some of them also provide discussion of the steps and follow-up interviews.

1. The Swish Pattern. The swish pattern is an amazingly rapid and powerful submodality intervention developed by Richard Bandler that is particularly generative. The first demonstration uses the standard swish on a simple habit, nail-biting. The client in the second demonstration went into uncontrolled rages when her daughter spoke in a certain voice tone. This contains an example of thorough testing to find out precisely which submodalities are powerful for the client, and designing an appropriate swish—in this case in the auditory system. (71 min., $65)

2. A Strategy for Responding to Criticism. This strategy, modeled by Steve and Connirae Andreas, allows a person to be open to feedback without experiencing bad feelings. A demonstration of installing this strategy is followed by discussion and a follow-up interview. (40 min., $50)

3. "The Last Straw" Threshold Pattern. Richard Bandler first modeled how people go "Never again!" with unsatisfying relationships, situations, or personal habits. The Andreas demonstrate eliciting this pattern, followed by a discussion of a number of different examples. Recommended for those with prior NLP training. (60 min., $50)

4. Shifting the Importance of Criteria. A "workaholic" is helped to decrease the importance of work, and increase the importance of personal needs. An 18-month follow-up interview details the scope of the resulting changes. (31 min., $50)

5. The Fast Phobia/Trauma Cure. An intense 20-year phobia of bees is eliminated in six minutes, using the fast phobia/trauma cure developed by Richard Bandler. An 11-month follow-up interview with the client is included, as well as a 15-minute follow-up interview with a Vietnam veteran whose "post-traumatic stress syndrome" lasting 12 years was also completely changed in one session using this method. (42 min., $50)

189

6. Changing Beliefs. The submodalities belief change pattern developed by Richard Bandler is demonstrated in an Advanced Submodalities Training. An explanation accompanies the demonstration, which is followed by questions, discussion, and preparation for a hands-on exercise using the pattern. A three-month follow-up interview with the client is also included. (104 min., $85)

7. Future-Pacing: Programming Yourself to Remember Later. How people program themselves to remember something automatically in the future is explored in this session taken from the second day of a 24-day Practitioner Training in January, 1985. (79 min., $65)

These videotapes of NLP Training sessions and/or NLP work with individuals were produced by Connirae and Steve Andreas. Other videotapes are in production: write for current list. All tapes are also available in the European PAL system at the same price, plus shipping.

If you order any three (or more) videotapes, you can receive 15% discount. (This includes NLP/CO Bandler videotapes listed in Appendix II.) ($7.50 off a $50 tape, $10.00 off a $65 tape, and $13.00 off an $85 tape). All prices are postpaid (special 4th class book rate) within the U.S. First-Class and Airmail postage is extra.

Please indicate whether you want VHS or Beta format. Foreign Orders: indicate U.S. NTSC system or European PAL system. Send order with payment to:

NLP Comprehensive
1221 Left Hand Canyon Dr.
Boulder, CO 80302
(303) 442-1102

Appendix II

Richard Bandler Videotapes

A. Client Sessions
Richard Bandler demonstrates clinical applications of NLP methods in three half-hour studio-quality tapes with clients. (Transcripts of these sessions appear in the book *Magic in Action*.)

1. Anticipatory Loss. A woman who experienced disabling panic attacks whenever someone close to her was late for an appointment is cured of her problem.

2. Authority Figures. A young man is helped to overcome his fear of authority figures.

3. Agoraphobia. A middle-aged truck driver is cured of his six-year inability to leave the city limits of the town he lives in.

Each tape shows the entire unedited session with these clients, none of whom had previously met Richard, and all three tapes include a follow-up session demonstrating the success of the session. The price for each session is $75, or $150 for all three sessions on one tape (VHS format only). Make checks payable to: Marshall University Foundation (No postage or handling charges.) Order from: Dr. Virginia Plumley, Marshall University, Huntington, WV 25701, (304) 523-0080.

B. An Introduction to Submodalities
This 3½ hour, two-videotape set was edited from an introductory submodalities seminar in San Diego in early 1987. $179 postpaid, VHS format only.

Order from: NLP Products and Promotions, P.O. Box 1756, Aptos, CA 95001-1756. (408) 684-1563.

C. Submodalities and Hypnosis
These videotapes were edited from a comprehensive four-day advanced submodalities seminar in Boulder, Colorado in early 1987. The titles and descriptions below only point out major themes in this thorough and systematic training. Since Richard is always demonstrating while he is teaching, these tapes provide an exceptionally rich experience of current submodalities methods.

1. Amplifying Kinesthetic States and Body Work. Richard teaches how to use nonlinear submodality relationships to amplify desired kinesthetic states and future-pace these states into appropriate contexts, with specific reference to sexual functioning. He also demonstrates his unique form of body work, which he developed out of his observation of the work of Moshe Feldendrais and others. (117 min., $85)

2. Nonverbal Elicitation and Change. Demonstrations, discussion, and exercises for using nonverbal anchoring, presuppositions, and sensory acuity to gather submodality information and make covert changes. (78 min., $65)

3. Presuppositions and Hypnosis. How presuppositions change submodalities, and the direct use of submodality shifts to induce altered states. (63 min., $50)

4. Redesigning and Chaining States. Utilizing the submodalities of time to install attitudes, mood states, and behaviors that are inevitable because they have subjectively already happened, and the use of trance and finger signals for unconscious installation and contextualization. (96 min. $85)

5. Convictions, Beliefs, and Reality. Working with beliefs, convictions, and reality strategies to make lasting changes. Using submodalities to separate states or to synthesize new states. (82 min. $65)

You can order the complete set of five videotapes for $280 (a saving of 20%). Order from NLP Comprehensive (see the end of Appendix I for ordering information).

Several other videotapes are in production in September 1987 and will be available soon, including individual client sessions with an alcoholic, a paranoid schizophrenic, a bulimic, and a man who was shy with women. Write or call NLP Comprehensive for current list. (303) 442-1102.

D. Ericksonian Hypnosis Seminar Videotapes

This set of three videotapes totalling 4 hours, 15 minutes is edited from a weekend seminar that Richard Bandler taught with Ed Reese at the Southern Institute of NLP in 1986. Many applications of submodalities to hypnosis are demonstrated, as well as pattern interruption, metaphor, linguistic hypnotic patterns, arm levitation, double induction, and chaining states. They conclude with personal stories of experiences with Milton Erickson. $225 postpaid within the U.S. (VHS format only). Order from: Hypnosis Vo-Cal Productions, P.O. Box 533, Indian Rocks Beach, FL 34635, (813) 596-4891.

Selected Bibliography

From Real People Press:

Bandler, Richard. *Using Your Brain—for a CHANGE*. Real People Press, 1985 (cloth $11.00, paper $7.50).

Bandler, Richard; and Grinder, John. *Frogs into Princes*. Real People Press, 1979 (cloth $11.00, paper $7.50).

Bandler, Richard; and Grinder, John. *Reframing: Neuro-Linguistic Programming and the Transformation of Meaning*. Real People Press, 1982 (cloth $12.00, paper $8.50).

Grinder, John; and Bandler, Richard. *Trance-formations: Neuro-Linguistic Programming and the Structure of Hypnosis*. Real People Press, 1981 (cloth $12.00, paper $8.50).

Order from: Real People Press, Box F, Moab, UT 84532, (801) 259-7578. 40% Discount on orders of 10 or more books (any combination of titles).

From Meta-Publications:

Bandler, Richard. *Magic in Action*. Meta-Publications, 1985 (cloth $14.95).

Order from: Meta Publications, P.O. Box 565, Cupertino, CA 95014.

You can also order these books, as well as many other books, videotapes, and audiotapes and other NLP resources from: NLP products and Promotions, P.O. Box 1756, Aptos, CA 95001-1756, (408) 684-1563.

Index